Date Your Career
The Longest Relationship of Your Life

ALEXSANDRA SUKHOY, M.B.A.

Dear Megan,
Thank you for
the opportunity!
Enjoy the adventure!
Cheers,
-Alex

ISBN-13: 978-1543197204

ISBN-10: 1543197205

15 14 13 12 11 10 9 8 7 6 5 4 3 2 1

DEDICATION

I dedicate this book to my son, David. The future is yours, Kid.

And to all my students. This is for you.

"NEW DAY.
NEW WEEK.
NEW MONTH.
NEW YEAR.
NEW CAREER."

#CREATIVECADENCE

#DateYourCareer.
photo: a. sukhoy

CONTENTS

ACKNOWLEDGMENTS

At its core, this book is a Cleveland project.

I'm very grateful to Thomas Mulready for not just writing the Foreword to this book, but for also cutting me my first writing check. He graciously invited me to write the Career ToolBox for his CoolCleveland publication and allowed me to cover any topic I wanted. Thomas, you are a *mensch*.

This book also couldn't happen if it wasn't for Cleveland State University and the Monte Ahuja School of Business. As part time faculty, not only did the school's leaders and instructors, Dr. Whitman, Dr. Dixit, Dr. Ghosh, Dr. Gross and Kim Ruggeri, entrust me with over 1000 students, but when I went on sabbatical and then nearly two years later had my child they also stood by me in full support. My students, several of which then became clients, further entrusted me with their career paths. And to Chris Connelly, Paul Ibrahim, Rachel Pankiw and Eric N. Dunn, thank you for saying, "Yes" when I invited you to be part of this project. Your stories will move people.

To Brad Michael Fellows, a former student who then became my closest friend in C-Town and who stood by me not only during my pregnancy but has also since become the amazing Uncle Brad to my son.

To Deena Nyer Mendlowitz, the one person who single-handedly drove me to read my writing in public and who then taught me to laugh at my heart's biggest pain. Deena – I want your beautiful words in every book I write.

To Peter Lawson Jones, who not only generously gave of himself to my students on multiple occasions, but also taught those of us fortunate to be in the classroom that one Fall day in 2012 that critical business lesson behind political parties. You are an incredible leader and also someone I am lucky enough to call friend.

To Jessica Weese, we started as coworkers, then became close friends. I'll never forget that one cold December night at the Clifton Diner and I'll always remember the warm summer breeze at our last night at Ferris. You define loyalty, class, warmth and humor. Your vineyard is waiting.

To Bryan Ceja, the only non-Clevelander in this project, and yet a man whose global heart beats to the same rhythm as mine. You are my Brother from another Grandmother.

To my Family - Mom, Dad, Sis, Ken - without whom single parenthood would've been impossible and who decades ago engrained in me the American spirit of education, hard work and possibility: anything boys could do, I fearlessly took on and you cheered me on at every successful and failing attempt.

And, of course, to the City of Cleveland. You, my dear, have challenged my professional journey many times over, each time propelling me towards a new destination that never quite hit the radar till you pulled your 216 magic. You welcomed me as a fresh-faced M.B.A. and you then morphed me into an entrepreneur, writer, photographer, world traveler, career coach, educator and, ultimately, into a Mom.

That is your gift, Cleveland. You push until the truth comes out.

"Drummers don't write - or at least, that's what everybody believes." – Tony Williams

FOREWORD
BY THOMAS MULREADY, COOLCLEVELAND

For many readers of this book who already know Alexsandra Sukhoy, you are probably smiling right now. For the rest, you have no idea what you're in for.

Alex and I are both drummers, and not the kind who swish around with brushes. Not that there's anything wrong with that. But we hit hard, and when Alex speaks, you best listen.

I listened when she pitched an idea for a column in CoolCleveland at the tail end of the Great Recession called Career ToolBox that would be focused on helping people get their careers, and their lives, back on track. At the time, many, many people were in need of this advice. Unsurprisingly, they still are.

Unless you happen to be a client or a student of Alex's, you haven't had the benefit of hearing her speak her wisdom. Well, now, with this book, *Date Your Career: The Longest Relationship of Your Life*, you do.

What you do with this opportunity is up to you. But I would suggest you follow Alex's lead just like this:

- **Alex always hit her deadlines**: Early is the new on-time. Don't ask. Show up ready and show up early.

- **Alex always took advice**: Not without an argument, and not without processing it through her years of experience. But she never let a good piece of advice go to waste.

- **Alex always wrote thank you notes**: So buy your notes and stamps now, and get started. I use postcards with a Cleveland theme. But almost anything will make the right impression.

- **Alex has never given in to her fears**: Acknowledgment of your shortcomings is one thing. Letting them get the best of you is unacceptable.

- **Alex never stopped moving forward**: So get busy with this book and start understanding which way is forward.

- **Alex never gave up**: Like all my favorite people, she's fun to watch. And impossible to second guess.

You've taken the first crucial step by opening this book. Now your challenge is to see how far you can go with your dreams and your career.

I'll bet you can make it all the way.

Section 1 – The Career Coaching Backstory

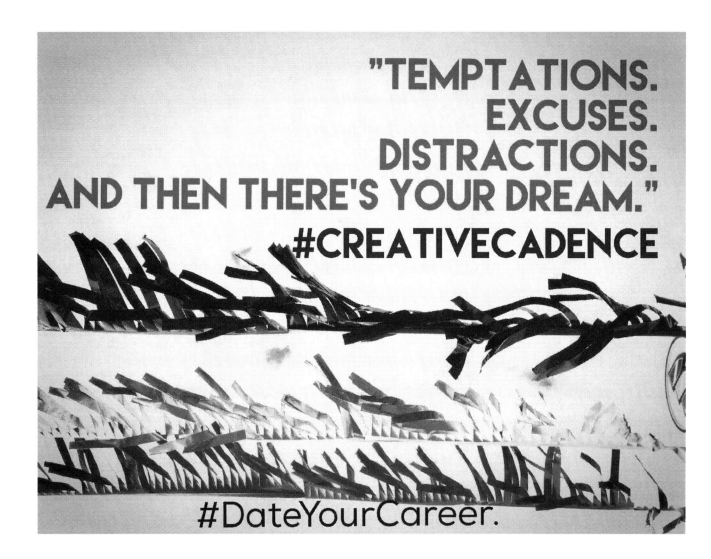

"TEMPTATIONS.
EXCUSES.
DISTRACTIONS.
AND THEN THERE'S YOUR DREAM."
#CREATIVECADENCE

#DateYourCareer.

"Genuine beginnings begin within us, even when they are brought to our attention by external opportunities."
— William Throsby Bridges

1.1
HOW IT ALL BEGAN

Over the years people have asked me, "How did you get into this?" And when they say "this" it could mean all kinds of things: Career Coaching, Entrepreneurship, Teaching or Writing.

Each story has its initial seed. That tiny nugget that, falling into the right soil, begins to take root. And the longer it stays there, the more stable the foundation it creates.

My background is purely Corporate America.

Business has always been part of my DNA and during high school graduation year, I was already working thirty hours a week at Old Orchard Shopping Center, in Skokie, Illinois, aka the Center of the Universe.

When I attended college at DePaul University in Chicago, I took on a full class load AND a full workload, hopping on 6am trains to make it to downtown and back. Throughout my college career, instead of Spring Breaks in Florida, fraternity parties and trips to Europe, my life consisted of earning my B+ GPA and earning an income to live on.

Work is what I knew. It's what I did.

Six years after graduating DePaul, and two Chicago company stints later, in late August 2001, when I started graduate school, at the University of Rochester Simon Business School, I had big dreams, big hopes and giant aspirations. I wanted to change the world.

Then two weeks into the program, the unthinkable happened: 9/11. From just a few hours away the impact at Ground Zero hurricaned its way all over the world.

5

On September 12, as the rest of the campus shut down, giving the opportunity for its students to grieve, bond and somehow makes sense of what occurred, we, the MBA students, had to be in our seats that morning, assignments completed, quiz-ready. Why? Because, we were told, "Markets never rest."

Shortly after, the market crashed. Along with all those dreams, hopes and aspirations. The attack blew the lids off corrupted firms such as Enron and Worldcom. The tech bubble imploded. And all that extra cash pumped into circulation in 1999 in fear of Y2K lost its prestige. And value.

And so here we were, several hundred hopeful MBAs, half international, trying to renavigate in a world at chaos. We did have each other and on each other we leaned, learning social phrases in different languages, sampling ethnic foods and dancing to diverse music. It was survival. Global style.

In 2002, I took on several roles in the school:

1. Team Coach, helping the incoming class adjust to their new pressures
2. Management Communication T.A., working with students on their written and oral correspondence styles
3. Writing Center Tutor, where I met with individuals and worked with them on their Resumes, Cover Letters and Mock Interviews, providing insight and feedback on how to make them strong and stand out in what still was a shitty job economy.

Additionally, I took on the role of Head Writer and Photographer with WATS, *The World According to Simon*, the magazine of the school. There I wrote on everything from songs about money to the reality of women's equality in the business arena, especially springing from a class that had only 22% of us women. I loved writing for the magazine and then also contributing endless photographs to our class yearbook.

And so, that is where it all began. Where the seed first planted itself in the Career Coaching platform.

Major General Sir William Throsby Bridges was right. Sometimes it is the external that drives our life's deltas. Our job? To listen, to not resist and to be open to where it leads. And then leads, again.

"There isn't any need to deny everything there's been just because you are going to lose it."
— Ernest Hemingway, For Whom the Bell Tolls

1.2
THE MENTOR CALLING RINGS TRUE

A corporate job offer prompted my move to Cleveland, Ohio, in Fall of 2003. Nestled on the shores of Lake Erie, Cleveland would be my third Great Lakes City in three years, following Chicago (Lake Michigan) and Rochester (Lake Ontario).

I worked very hard at my job. Late evenings, long work days, short weekends and abridged holidays. I earned every single cent I made there and for every social and personal opportunity I passed up. Deadlines, presentations, meetings, training sessions, interviews, Excel spreadsheets, it was all part of the MBA deal.

It's what no one tells you when you're in business school: that your opportunity cost for having those initials and all that student debt signaled a workhorse to the executives of Corporate America. This was the price you paid for a good salary, good benefits and three weeks of vacation time.

Sometimes I met the company expectations. Sometimes I didn't. Sometimes the expectations weren't clear or changed 100 times. No matter what, I worked hard. And paid attention.

Then around 2006 a couple of nice gentlemen I had befriended in my new home city reached out to me. Both were in their early/mid 20's. Both college-educated. Both ambitious. They each wanted to get into very particular MBA programs and asked for my help. Doing the Good Samaritan pay-it-forward thing, knowing that I didn't need their money, as I was gainfully employed, I took the time to work with each of them. Specifically, we focused on their Resumes and on their Application Essays. I was adamant about not writing any of these documents for either of them. Instead, they provided the raw material and I pushed them really hard on it. I mentored them through the entire process, beginning to end. The result? Each was accepted to his Ivy League MBA program of choice. Both on full scholarship. This certainly rang a bell. A loud one. But it would be another couple of years before I truly heard it.

"I'm the Bad Guy?…How'd that happen? I did everything they told me to."
– Bill Foster, Falling Down, 1993

1.3
2008 – THE BIG CRASH

2008 began as a terrific year. Just a couple months prior I shifted into a new job with the same company, the December right before I flew to Madrid, Spain to visit my Simon MBA colleague Gabriella and for the first time both my professional career and my creative pursuits found a good balance. Plus, between neighbor friends, work friends, Israel trip friends and local Simon Alumni friends (I'd started the Cleveland Alum Association when I first moved here), the social circle exploded. I found my groove. My creativity found its outlet.

Here in Cleveland I became the most authentic version of myself.

Then mid-year, around late summer, early fall 2008, something began to change. It changed at work. It changed at the market. And something began to trigger a directional shift that just felt off. When everything looks right, but feels wrong, you know the tsunami is coming.

I don't need to remind anyone of what happened next. The big 2008 market crash: Bernie Madoff stole, the over-inflated real estate marked imploded and jobs evaporated. Panic prevailed. Meanwhile our tax dollars bailed out the auto and bank industries because the previous and the new presidential administrations both felt that they were Too Big Too Fail. (Not that they were actually mismanaged.)

But what about the individuals? America's citizens that did all the right things throughout their careers: they earned their education, they worked hard, they saved. What happened to them? To us? We became irrelevant.

No one was going to bail out us.

I don't want to dwell too much on all the darkness that prevailed for the next several years. To say it was hard is an understatement. I, along with so many others, went into survival mode. And had to very quickly figure out how to be relevant again. Because the old formula? It no longer worked.

I began working full time when I was seventeen. And this was just two months before my thirty-seventh birthday. Twenty years I gave of myself to delivering profits to others. Two decades later, what was the reward for all my loyalty, including all those late nights, weekends, cancelled dates and Sunday night ulcers? Something inside me snapped. I had to take a step back and reevaluate everything. And I mean everything.

Who was I if I wasn't a corporate servant?

I had to rediscover my roots.

"Carry your cup in your hand, and look around
Leaves are brown, now, and the sky is a hazy shade of winter."
— Simon and Garfunkel

1.4
2009 – RENAVIGATING THE CHAOS

2009 proved to be an interesting year. Interesting is such a neutral adjective. On one hand, I began the year with some savings and a finite severance package. On the other hand I was also out of a job and in a new house with new mortgage payments. No one was hiring. Shady organizations prayed on people's fear. And the new Democratic presidential administration, voted in just two months prior and inheriting this mess, along with the debt of the previous Republican eight years, was simultaneously energetic and hopeful all the while inexperienced and naive.

Who was going to get us out of this mess? Surely not the politicians and definitely not the corporations. We were all on our own. And, those of us lucky enough to have good family, friends and neighbors, we also had each other. Suddenly at home dinner invitations spiked, generosity prevailed and it was the spirit and kindness of good people that gave others hope.

After a brutal and cruel winter, spring arrived and along with it a call from a fellow Simon MBA who started her own healthcare consulting business. She needed a video to articulate her research findings, saw my music video for a song I wrote called "Cleveland Rising" and offered me the project. Suddenly, I was a video producer! I immediately reached out to key technical people and quickly we got to work.

Also, a friend I'd known since grade school, and whom I've helped with his Resume previously, referred my first paying Career Coaching client. This man was a consultant, husband and father. And, after just three months of our work together, in 2009, in the midst of that crappy economy, he accepted an offer for a new job, one with more pay and less travel time. Then a close friend, an engineer, whom I took on pro-bono, gave me his Resume and shortly after, recruiters started calling him with multiple opportunities.

Something about the work I was doing with people quickly led them to desired results. So I kept going.

Creative Cadence, the content firm I had started back in 2007, now became my one-stop agency. Its branding?

Where Commerce and Culture Converge.

That year a former coworker contacted me and made an introduction with a woman named Kim. Kim taught full time at the CSU Business School and was looking for guest speakers to come into the classroom and to speak with the students on business, marketing and careers. So I volunteered. And for multiple semesters in a row, would volunteer a full day and speak to 2 – 3 large classes on the truth of what to expect during the job hunt process and then what will be expected of them once they accept those offers. My tone with each group was direct and honest. No sugar coating.

Corporate America is hard work.

A year prior to the crash while still gainfully employed, inspired by the events surrounding the Cavs/Pistons championship series in Cleveland and by the James cover of Leonard Cohen's epic ballad of the same name, began writing a script originally called "So Long, Marianne." Just two weeks prior to my job loss it was due to Cleveland's Film Commissioner. A few months later, in Spring of 2009 I received a call from him. He read my screenplay. And sent me to Cinestory, a hard-core industry-intensive screenwriting seminar in the mountains, just outside Los Angeles. An alumni retreat, full of film major students and film producer mentors, I showed up as the underdog.

My script? Fully dismantled. And yet, I still got up there, pitched new ideas, networked like crazy and made some key connections that still influence my writing today.

By the time fall of 2009 arrived, I was personally recruited to take over another instructor's Art of Story class at Cuyahoga Community College, Creative Cadence began to earn a good reputation with clients and two different online publications, CoolCleveland and *Film Slate*, opened their contributor doors to me.

The Coaching, Writing, Teaching trifecta emerged.

"Struggle is struggle and what I learned during my speaking engagements – really conversations – is that sometimes the only way people will connect with you is if they feel the depth of your struggle matches theirs."
– A. S.

1.5
2010 & 2011 – A NEW PROFESSIONAL CHAPTER

Teaching began to take center stage. I didn't go to college or graduate school to study education or how to be an educator. However, I took quite naturally to it and the students, at least most of them, seemed to connect with me.

After two decades of propelling products and profits, I was finally propelling people. And this I loved.

Late spring/early summer of that year, I reached out to my friend Kim, the one who teaches at CSU, and asked if there were any teaching opportunities available. My timing couldn't have been any better. Given various perfect storm circumstances,

I was hired to teach my first class at CSU.

It was remote, at the Progressive Insurance facility on the far east side, and while it was nerve-wrecking at first, it also tapped into all the things I'd done for over twenty years: the understanding of how business works, what Corporate America's expectations are of its workforce and the critical importance of public speaking. And so I passed this knowledge on to my students. In the best way I could.

That fall, I taught three classes at Tri-C, Business Environment at CSU and, mid-semester, took over Kim's three Marketing classes. I'd never be allowed to teach seven classes at one school, but between the two, I took whatever work I could. Work meant money and money meant paying bills.

That fall I also had to make a giant decision. Three years after making the biggest mistake of my life, I had to finally confront it. In business there's something called a death spiral – it's when you keep investing into something that isn't giving anything back to you. It just keeps taking with zero promise of any return.

My house was that death spiral. And after doing all I could to do what's right and whatever was legally and fiscally possible, it reached a point of no return. It was a sunk cost.

And, so, that November, with the help of family and friends I packed up and moved out. And faced the implications of that move. Instead of viewing the walk-away a failure, I made the life decision that businesses constantly make in order to keep going. Playing life by the book, I just got there three years after I should have.

But then. No one declared me too big to fail.

No one was going to bail me out.

"I did not believe the information, I just had to trust imagination."
– Peter Gabriel

1.6
2012 – A WELCOME FRESH START

2012 began with life in a new, beautiful apartment, two teaching gigs, two online writing gigs and two book pursuits. Two seemed like the magical number. Additionally, the Career Coaching clientele began to build and life, for the first time in three years, felt peaceful.

One of the big trends I began to notice in my business is that clients no longer came from just the Corporate America/Consulting arena. By this point, I was working with people from all kinds of sectors: Education, Media and Transitioning Military. Additionally, various women who weren't sure how to handle the next step of their career, reached out because they simply felt lost.

By this time I had developed and optimized a series of Career Coaching Assessment Tools; proprietary exercises that helped clients zone in and focus on what mattered most. And these Assessment Tools began to work. Some women stayed in their current roles, some shifted out of corporate and into non-profit and one had a baby. Finally, a couple of former students began to reach out as they needed Resume help.

As I transitioned my life, discontent adults turned to me to help them transition.

They knew my story and trusted me with theirs.

And so the year progressed, full of healthy momentum, though Fall. And during Fall, always my personal season of change, things began to feel odd, both personally and with one of my teaching gigs. Back in January I had already quit contributing to the online film publication because, well, after two years of no pay, the free movie passes no longer mattered all that much. And the access to major cinema events dwindled. I'd done a pretty good job of networking with some Hollywood talent and have maintained those relationships, including my support of their craft, in an ongoing basis. And working for free just to possibly meet more felt absurd.

But there was something bigger than that going on. 2012 was the year that I finally began to feel my worth, again.

Yes, it took three long years since that painful corporate exit to not just rediscover who I was, but, more importantly, to comprehend, consciously and subconsciously, that the projects you say yes to when you're feeling low and insecure end up costing you far more of your life than the projects and jobs you say yes to when you know exactly just how much your contribution matters.

The tremendous 1946 film noir, *The Postman Only Rings Twice*, has a powerful quote: "Guaranteed poverty is not job security." And a lot of what I allowed into my life, with full pursuit, during 2009, 2010 and 2011, was anchored in that guaranteed poverty. Yes, exceptions occurred, like all those fantastic, yet temporary corporate gigs. And, as anyone who has ever started a business knows that in the beginning you reward the people who take a risk on you – whether via pro bono work or deeply discounted services or free samples. You must give people a reason to try you. There was a lot of that giving.

Finally, beyond the whole cost benefit equation of time and resources vs. reward and payment, one critical element began to surface in 2012, first quietly and then ringing like a giant church bell. And that was how certain people treated me.

Between the end of 2012 and the first half of 2013, I quit allocating energy to people who did not respect mine. So I said good-bye to teaching film studies, reviewing films and a personal relationship.

I use the line, "markets never rest" a lot. It was my first lesson at business school. It also applies to every facet of our lives because the nature of human condition is forward motion.

In the first true modern romantic comedy *Annie Hall* (1977), Woody Allen says the following brilliant line, "A relationship is like a shark. It has to constantly move forward or it dies."

By the end of 2012 several of my relationships began to wither off. For they no longer served a place in my forward motion. In fact, they simply slowed me down.

And I had other plans.

"He came dancing across the water, with his galleons and guns
Looking for the new world, in that palace in the sun."
– Neil Young

1.7
2013 – SINKING SHIPS, CORTÉS STYLE

2013 built on the loss of 2012. And more was to follow. Pruning the dead leaves of one's life is a critical component to letting the healthy seeds blossom. Making space for the new is not an option. It's evolution.

I continued to teach at CSU and my Career Coaching biz grew to include even more clients, from more industries and with even more varied experience. Word of mouth grew. People trusted me. Their results proved to be Creative Cadence's best marketing.

I also noticed a trend with my clients. The quicker and more compliant they were with the work we did together, the quicker and better their results. Those who hesitated or dragged the process out – regardless of whatever professional or personal priorities had to take place instead – well, they didn't quite experience the delta of the compliant ones. I'm not to judge anyone's decision. And I'm always, ALWAYS, grateful for every single client that hires me. Call it energy, call it momentum, but the laser-focused approach continues to trump the more relaxed one.

As the first half of 2013 progressed, I noticed all kinds of changes, from within and in the mirror. While I never started any sort of short-lived diet or quit eating any of the many things people tell you not to eat, the commitment to the gym and, perhaps ending that relationship, shifted my entire life regime. As I worked out more, I slept much better through the night. As I slept better, I craved less food. As I craved less food, my body began to adjust to consuming less calories. And, so, by mid-May, I had dropped twenty pounds. I've never pulled this off before. And I didn't have to quit eating anything. People noticed. People complimented. Old clothes began to fit. My breathing was better. My life felt better. I felt better. And rewarded myself with a cool new hairstyle, metaphorically cutting off ~ 6″ – or a year's worth – of hair and adding a bold pink stripe to the front.

The summer of 2013 created another pivoting moment. I wasn't going to be teaching any classes that summer. Part of me panicked – while not a large salary for us contract workers, knowing that each semester you knew you were going to get paid, you knew when and you knew how much, was the perfect beta-balancer to entrepreneurship. I had to truly take a step back and provide myself with the confidence that I could do this. That four and a half years since working for a corporation I can sustain myself with my own business. And sustain myself I did.

That summer, for the first time, my company went international as three different clients from Canada hired me for my services. Additionally, a huge marketing agency from Chicago hired me to do an industry research project. And between all that revenue, plus the ongoing writing for the local publication and steady stream of clients, that summer I felt independent. I felt confident. I felt free.

And, if you're anything like me, when things get too comfortable, you begin to feel itchy. As I stood my ground during the years of the job loss and then the house loss and then the relationship loss and then began to rediscover who the new me was without all these things, I began to get a little bored. Of course I loved my work. I loved my friends. And I loved my writing. But beyond that? The bigger life in the smaller body felt constricted. I needed change.

So I called my Skokie childhood friend Melanie Klinghoffer, with whom we always joke we share parallel lives, and asked her for help. I even wrote a blog about it: "Who Coaches a Career Coach's Career?" I needed an unbiased, pragmatic and actionable perspective on how to make key changes all the while preserving my new self. It was also the first time in many years that I genuinely began to rethink that Cleveland was home.

From January till ~ June of 2013, I lived 6 months in a monastic lifestyle: work, work out, write, sleep, repeat. Once in a while I'd go out with friends, but, mostly, I was like a bear in hibernation, in my own woman cave, shutting off the noise of the world and staying away from all temptation. From 2009 to 2012, the volatility of things – of everything – took its toll and I had to just go in and see what person would re-emerge.

The Summer of 2013 found me lighter – in pounds, in personal space and in commitments. It also became the transition before everything expedited to completion. Like that split second when you throw a ball in the air and it stops and spins before falling back down, July and August, were my moments in the air.

While I went on some dates and met some interesting people, personal relationships didn't really matter in 2013. They weren't the priority. I had to put it all behind me. Why didn't the men matter as much as they once did? Because in the summer of 2013 I decided that it was time to leave Cleveland and move to a new city.

The time had come. I fought for this. And no man or company or anything or anyone was going to get in my way.

Not this time.

I had five requirements for my future city:

1. Warm climate
2. No state taxes
3. Robust economy
4. Thriving creative scene
5. Ocean view

After exploring various cities, I narrowed in to Austin, Texas. Four out of five on my list – only criteria missing was the ocean view. Allegedly Austin is the coolest city in America. And, so, while I continued life as usual, I also knew that my time in Cleveland was finite.

One of the biggest gifts of the previous four years was the dedication to developing a business that was totally independent of geography. Sure, technology provided a certain freedom – have laptop, smart phone, internet? You're all set. Even deeper, psychologically and subconsciously, a part of me wanted to ensure that I'd never have to depend on anyone or anything for my income. Not only was the Creative Cadence biz model lean – no partner, no employees, very few physical supplies and only hire subcontractors on a project-by-project basis – it was (and still is) a very green operation. Besides the technology tools mentioned, I get to run it with minimal supplies: journals, Sharpies, printer and file folders. That's it. No office space to rent, no equipment to maintain, no inventory to ship.

I wanted to specialize in what I wanted to do: Coach, Teach and Write. Exchange ideas. Facilitate thoughts. Challenge expectations.

That summer my grad school, Simon Business, had an alumni event at the Ritz in Downtown Cleveland. It was great seeing all the local talent sharing the Rochester roots. Even the Simon School (former) Dean, Mark Zupan, came in. He asked me how life was. I replied to him, "Well, by end of December, beginning of January, my apartment lease, car lease and semester contract all expire."

"Oh," he replied. "So you're Cortés. And you're sinking your ships."

And Cortés I was. In the chaotic month of December, I sold or donated all my furniture, wrapped up teaching two of my classes plus the four I took over when Kim went on another maternity leave, said my emotional goodbyes to the tremendous friends I made in Cleveland, moved out of my building and ended all my ties with the city that, for a decade was home.

But not before a few funny things happened. Earlier in the semester, I'd lost my CSU office keys and when the department admin returned me the found pair, she attached them to a key chain in the shape of a little house.

And, because of the nasty blizzard, I ended up crashing with my friends Daniel and Hannah for a few days. They (along with two other sets of contacts) also generously agreed to let me leave some of my remaining stuff/personal items in their basement and together we celebrated New Year's Eve, welcoming in 2014 in the 216.

On January 2, the temperature was so cold that it would not snow. So I packed up my VW, hit 90 and with Cleveland in my rear view mirror, headed west, committed to never look back. I sunk my ships. Time had finally come to explore new lands.

"Tropical the island breeze, all of nature wild and free
This is where I long to be, La isla bonita."
— Madonna

1.8
2014 – THE SABBATICAL

2014 stands as one of the greatest years of my life. I lived the first six months of it couch surfing six cities in three countries and two continents.

I've written plenty on the experience and there's probably never enough words to fully express everything I felt, everyone I met and all the places and things I saw. It truly was a once in a lifetime. It was my once in a lifetime.

My calendar was as follows:

• January: Chicago, IL
• February: Dublin, Ireland
• 1-week Midwest Intermission in Chicago, then Cleveland
• March: Coral Springs, FL
• April: Austin, TX
• May: Cancun, Mexico
• June: Cleveland (still couch surfing)
• July: Lakewood, finally home in my current apartment

In each of these cities I continued to work and extend my client base. I also wrote about experiences that are still hard to comprehend. The highlights? Meeting and having the now late John Hurt sign my writer's journal at the Dublin Internal Film Festival and three months later watching my Sister and Brother in Law walk down the aisle together.

During those six months I cleared my head, healed my heart, replenished my fuel and renavigated life into a completely different direction. And understood that I feel most at home both across the pond and in the Midwest but never in the South.

When I returned to Cleveland, I knew that everything within me shifted and something really big was going to happen. I just wasn't sure what that would be.

And as I resumed my trifecta of teaching, coaching writing, while I was doing the same things in the same city that thought I had left for good, what wasn't the same was who I was.

The Career Coaching business thrived. CSU welcomed me back with open arms. And my forth book, *Diary of the Dumped*, received the biggest press attention of all my projects: blog, magazine, newspaper, radio and television coverage and interviews. It even made it into the Sunday Arts section. Multiple book readings. Library distribution. Phenomenal Amazon reviews. It hit a certain note with women and men alike.

All of me was ready for the next big thing.

"If I could only see one miracle, just one miracle. Like a burning bush, or the seas part, or my uncle Sasha pick up a check."
– Woody Allen

1.9
2015 – THE MIRACLE

2015 began on a strange note. I couldn't quite comprehend some actions of some people. And I certainly couldn't reconcile how the new and improved me couldn't immediately recognize and filter the broken in others. And yet, out of all the confusion and chaos came creation.

One year after I returned from my sabbatical I discovered I was pregnant. I was in shock. Who gets pregnant for the very first time in their life at the ripe age of 43?

And so, the second half of 2015 I juggled teaching, coaching and writing and carrying a healthy and big baby to full term. My students acted with the utmost respect as I entered a physically bigger person with each week's class. I told my clients, some of them, and they were great about it.

Mostly, in a city with no blood family and where I spent most of my pregnancy alone, I made sure I stayed healthy and calm, for myself and for my baby.

On December 24, 2015, nine days ahead of schedule, I gave birth to David Gabriel. A healthy, happy, thriving and beautiful boy. He's the love of my life.

As a Single Mom, I was back at work within two weeks of his birth and am blessed to be able to mostly work from home. I'm typing these words to you right now from my living room as D naps in his.

Juggling life has been no easy task. However, my twenty years in Corporate America – staying organized, anticipating my bosses' demands and keeping emotions even keeled – is what prepared me for motherhood. I never read any baby books or attended any prenatal classes. I also didn't grow up in a house with babies – I was the youngest in my immediate family. And, yet, my managerial experience gave me the foundation for a demanding boss whose body language I had to decipher from Day 1.

In almost every job I've ever had, with the most minor exception, I had female bosses: strong and smart women, many who became mothers while I worked for them, and who pushed me to be better, smarter, faster. To all of them, I say, Thank You!

My teaching experience taught me the art of patience and repetition.

My writing experience made sure that I kept a diary during pregnancy so that one day my son can know about his journey to this earth.

My entire professional career is what shaped me as a mother. And each morning, as I feed my kid, I read him the *Wall Street Journal* headlines. I don't know if he understands anything I'm reading to him. And that's ok.

He is my favorite CEO.

ALEXSANDRA SUKHOY

Section 2 – Career Advice

"No one else is responsible for your career."

#MarchForward

#CREATIVECADENCE

STRATEGY. MARKETING. COACHING.

FOR THE GRAD

"Well, it's very comfortable just to drift here."
- Dustin Hoffman, The Graduate

"Skill is fine, and genius is splendid, but the right contacts are more valuable than either."
– Arthur Conan Doyle, Sr.

2.1
YOU'VE GRADUATED. NOW WHAT?

While there's no substitute for working hard and earning a respectable GPA, there's one key responsibility that college grads must take on and the earlier in their education process, the better: networking.

The key is, obviously, to get started as early as possible.

The aggressiveness may seem over the top, but with at least five other people competing for the same spot, long gone are the days of viewing a college degree as a career insurance policy.

During the networking process, make sure to use all the tools available. In addition to social media (Facebook, LinkedIn, Twitter), have pre-printed business cards that provide your contact information and a short title or statement that says something about yourself, so that people can identify you with an industry or skill set. Also, include a professional head shot as part of the card and, for consistency, use the same photo on your LinkedIn page, blog, website, etc. Join professional associations and don't limit your connections to the virtual world – go out there and physically meet people.

Another important idea to keep in mind is karma. Realize that while people want to help you succeed, the networking and relationship building must work both ways. If a professor has done something meaningful for you, write them a LinkedIn recommendation. Send thoughtful thank you notes to people who have extended a hand. Offer your help to people who are climbing up behind you. The reciprocity builds an energy and, long term, people will know that they can count on you.

Additionally, and specifically regarding Gen Y and their helicopter parents, have the people looking for the job do their own homework. At a certain point, it's time to let go and let the kids make their own mistakes, all part of growing up and becoming an adult.

It's a tremendous turn-off to perspective employers when parents show up in interview rooms. Graduating college is a right of passage, and, even in a tough economy, it calls for tremendous independence and self-navigation.

Regardless of where you are in the process – in college, recent graduate or in a graduate program – the biggest contribution you can make to the success of your job placement is showcasing your talents to others via frequent and sincere communication. This is your life. What are you going to do with it?

"She works hard for the money, so hard for it honey."
— Donna Summer

2.2
HOW THE MBA SHAPED MY CREATIVE CAREER

At a time when big business is getting such a bad rep and when there's a completely unnecessary national divide — bankers vs. artists, religious vs. atheists, urbanites vs. bucolics, marrieds vs. singles, Boomers vs. Millennials, vegetarians vs. meatatarians, bicyclists vs. SUVers — it's good to know that some pursuits can help you reconcile life, regardless of desired achievements.

At a 2013 Cleveland Alumni event for University of Rochester, Simon School, the school's Dean at the time, Mark Zupan, personally invited me to come speak to the current students. As he's one of the five people outside my family circle who can ask me for anything, the last weekend of September I hopped into my car and drove out to beautiful Upstate New York.

My brief visit there was a whirlwind of events and tremendous networking opportunities. Of course, I reconnected with fellow classmates, which is always a terrific experience. Everyone's made a tremendous impact in the world of business, including in healthcare, technology and grocery industries — as well as balancing that majestically with family and kids. These are good people making a positive contribution to our economy and truly exemplifying leadership that's felt across the whole country. It was great to see everyone's smiles, especially since it's been about a decade since I saw some of these folks.

That Friday, I also had some quality time with Mark, spoke to a room full of ambitious business students about how social media impacts their personal branding and, after all that, joined former Simon teammate and great friend Rami Katz at a high-tech conference, where, as COO of Excell Partners Inc., he spoke on how start-up firms must behave in order to generate funding. It was all a huge thrill ride; since my corporate exit five years ago, this high-adrenaline environment is no longer part of my day-to-day. And while I don't foresee myself knocking on a corporation's door anytime soon, this weekend visit was that perfect jolt that reminded me why I went to business school to begin with.

Looking back now, I realize so many seeds of my creative career today were planted over a decade ago, in that complex time when I arrived in New York State, just two weeks before 9/11 changed everything. It's no secret that the first year of classes and the surrounding pressures tested every ounce of my being. So one day I took out a piece of paper and with a Sharpie wrote down why I was even there: "I am earning my MBA so that one day I can profit off of my own creativity." I then taped that piece of paper on the wall next to my desk, as a daily reminder of the goal.

During Spring of 2002, the tide shifted, I found my groove and began to get involved. I applied and earned the role of head writer of the school's newspaper. I absolutely adored writing for the quality publication and while it wasn't my entry into the craft, it was the first time my craft had a wide audience. At that time I was also hired by the Career Management Center to work with students on their resumes, cover letters, interviews and communication skills. Additionally, I applied and was hired to be a Team Coach for the first year students, helping them navigate the business school landscape. Guiding others towards their career goals felt very natural and intuitive.

Finally, I had the opportunity to learn from some of the most brilliant and loyal minds on the planet. My Simon professors challenged our collective thinking and ensured that we learned how to view business problems in ways that were new for many of us. They prepared us to look through multiple angles and to anticipate as many outcomes. Mostly, they taught us to think ten steps ahead, because someone is always building a better mouse trap.

Today, my professional career requires me to coach, teach and write. I chose this creative path and I love that each one of these functions builds off of and helps the other two evolve. My students are constantly pushing me to be better and to know more. My clients keep me on pulse with what's happening within the walls of Corporate America and my readers share with me which pieces resonate and which ones require a more genuine voice.

Today, everything I do builds on the experience I had at the Simon School. And as I shared with its current student body, the three career tools they will build — way beyond any specific subject they study — are problem solving, negotiation and a first class international network that they will carry for life.

It is fully possible to be an MBA with a creative career. It's not contradictory. It's actually a perfectly reconciled fit.

"I can never read all the books I want."
— Sylvia Plath,

2.3
5 BOOKS TO BOOST A GRADUATE'S CAREER:
READ YOUR WAY TO THE TOP

With lots of graduates entering the workforce and with new job openings springing to life, now's a great time to dig into smart books that will help boost your career. Each week Amazon seems to showcase hundreds of new self-help, how-to and business titles, all promising a new, rich life full of success and money.

The process to make the choice to read the right, most influential book that will influence our lives in a positive way can be overwhelming. What's actionable for some will be absurd for others. What's relatable for you can be a total disconnect for a friend.

To be clear, none of the books I included on this list came out this year and I read most of them prior to 2014. But, I have thought about them, referenced them or leaned on them frequently. Their wisdom is timeless and, if you've recently graduated and are open to post-textbook discovery, these authors and their words and advice will lead you down a good professional path.

• *The Real Life MBA* by Suzy and Jack Welch – Here's the deal. If you're thinking of earning your MBA I promise you Jack Welch will be a case. Or a chapter. Or an exam. He's the Greatest CEO of the 20th Century. And he and his wife and life partner, Suzy Welch, the former editor of the Harvard Business Review, wrote this book together. In Spring 2014 (when I was already pregnant but didn't yet know) I got to see them speak and then met them in person. Suzy's work/life balance (it's a myth!) practical advice is priceless. She will tell you how it really is.

• *Oh, The Places You'll Go* by Dr. Seuss – Whether a recent college grad or someone looking to shift how they earn a living, Dr. Seuss, with his perfect tempo rhyme and comforting wisdom, steers our inner child through the complex world of the unknown. It is only by exploring risk, with no helicopter parents to rescue you, that develops your character.

• *Outliers: The Story of Success* by Malcolm Gladwell – In an age of instant gratification Gladwell presents case study after case study of why certain individuals became the mega success that they are. You want to be a well known industry leader? Put in your 10,000 hours. As in do the work, every single day, for hours upon hours and don't expect any ribbons for doing so.

• *Execution: The Discipline of Getting Things Done* by Larry Bossidy and Ram Charam with Charles Burck – I've written about this title before, and for good reason. We can talk about our ideas all day. We can even complain how someone else isn't being respectful to our thoughts. But, bottom line, it's the doing of things that generates results. Put action before words. Watch the magic happen.

• *The Daily Drucker: 366 Days of Insight and Motivation for Getting the Right Things Done* by Peter Drucker – The original Godfather of corporate management, this man had the wherewithal to understand that recruiting, hiring, training and mentoring quality talent to do what's right vs. what's easy is, above all, the way to generate long-term success. Read his daily nuggets of wisdom daily, do what he says and others will quickly take notice.

Photo: a. sukhoy. Dublin. 2014.

Launch yourself beyond expectations.

#MarchForward

#CREATIVECADENCE
STRATEGY. MARKETING. COACHING.

GETTING STARTED

"You can bend the rules plenty once you get to the top, but not while you're trying to get there. And if you're someone like me, you can't get there without bending the rules." – Melanie Griffith, Working Girl

"I-Am-number one. No matter if you like it." - Nelly, Number 1

3.1
YOUR #1 PRIORITY

The greatest probability you give yourself to finding the right job is making finding that right job your #1 priority.

That will mean making some tough choices and giving some things a break - temporarily - till you're doing what you want. Unless you're clearing your calendar of everything else, you're gambling your chances going up against candidates with laser focus & killer determination.

"It's supposed to be hard. If it wasn't hard, everyone would do it. The hard…is what makes it great."
– Tom Hanks, A League of Their Own

3.2
ENTERING OPPORTUNITIES:
GETTING TO YOUR CAREER BASELINE

Determining one's occupational path is never simple. When we are in high school, the parental insistence to attend a quality college and determine an employable major corners us into a pressure cooker, driving decisions that may negate themselves in the future, when we have greater self-reliance.

However, even with a certain freedom, financial obligations, often in the form of debt – school loans, car loans, credit cards – deepen the dependence on chasing jobs-for-money vs. jobs-for-passion.

And, the older we get, the growing responsibilities we may bear – mortgages, children, parents or those pesky students loans – create the ball-and-chain effect where work's become not only the necessary prison to responsibly care for our life's overhead, but also the access provider to the ever-eroding health care system.

To be clear, I'm neither advising anyone to spontaneously quit a job that six other candidates are currently fighting for on this very day, nor can I, or anyone else, determine your tolerance for risk.

However, I am encouraging you to step back and think about what makes your heart happy, how you currently earn your paycheck and determine the gap between the two.

If you are professionally content, you are one of the few. Congratulations. If, looking back fifteen years, you envisioned something completely different, now is your time to take action.

Below is a process I work on with some of clients, which will help you get started:

1. "What did you used to lose yourself in when you were four years old?" Because your inner four-year old knew what you wanted to do and what made you curious.
2. "Make a list of ten things you love to do, not taking money nor skill set into consideration."
3. "Make a list of ten things at which you are very good."
4. "Take number 2 and number 3 and create a Venn diagram – see what overlaps."
5. This is your first indication of what is possible.

You now have your Career Baseline – the starting point of an intricate process that will help guide you to your life's calling. Take a deep breath and prepare yourself with all the energy-infusing support you know. The path won't be easy. Nothing worth anything good ever was.

"Hey! Get over here and see if you can get this toolbox off me!" – *Woody, Toy Story*

3.3
BRIDGING THE GAP:
ENTERING YOUR CAREER TOOLBOX

Now that you've developed your Career Baseline, it's time to focus on equipping yourself with the proper ammunition to know as much as possible about your desired industry. Because of the internet, information is readily available, yet puts the responsibility on the reader to decipher between fact and fiction, between quality and crap.

And, if your ultimate goal is to become an expert at something, early on determine where to start seeking the right data. If the world is one giant resource, then your job is to hone in on people, places and things that will help you bridge the gap between where you are today and where you want to be. As Rami Katz, a Simon school colleague, military vet, attorney and, currently, Director of Technology Commercialization at High Tech Rochester, once wisely told me, "Envision your goal and work backwards. Effort is over-rated. It's all about results."

Submerging yourself into your desired sector can be accomplished on several levels, including, but not limited to, education, training, reading and interaction – all four bring unique benefits. You'd do yourself a great service by assessing your own barometer with each. You may even want to break these out into a scale, label them 1 – 10 and mark where you are per category as it relates to your career goal. Then, determine your resources – time and money – to prioritize your energy spending: Now, Next and Later. Businesses do this with growth plans because even with deep pockets, not every pursuit is important and the combination of adaptability and discipline is key.

- **Study** - Over the past decade, higher learning has evolved into a very flexible arena. From on-line universities to rapidly expanding jr. colleges and even weekend grad schools, academia has recognized the growing interest of adults pursuing new skills and has responded with an increasing menu of class and program options. It's the basic economic model of supply and demand. Remember, not all schools hold equal footing. With whatever program you choose, weigh in on the network externalities – will the caliber of current students, alumni and the school's reputation open doors for you in the future?

- **Work** - In addition to the classroom, you will need hands-on experience. If you want to own your own flower shop, go work in a flower shop. There's a big difference between thinking you know how a business operates vs. learning from real life mistakes and victories. Whether full-time, part time, apprentice or intern work, any of these will help you assess if you even want to be in that business space. So start pounding the pavement and be grateful to anyone who will take a risk on you. Learn, work hard and spend at least all four seasons in one place to fully understand the life cycle of the organization's productivity model.

- **Read** - To compliment any classes you enroll in, make sure you're at the top of the industry trends by reading reputable publications within your desired arena. If your budget is tight, your librarian can help navigate you towards your specific needs. Regardless of your chosen trade, you will want to invest in an online subscription to the Wall Street Journal. With expanded coverage, it's the go-to source, not just for corporate executives, but also for anyone who wants to be on-pulse with everything from fine wine to political updates and even the arts. Also, make a list of leaders who've inspired you and read their bios, books and interviews. Observe the common patterns of success and see how you can apply them to yourself.

- **Network** - Finally, think of anyone and everyone that's in a related field and call, write and email them and ask them for five minutes of their time, because, chances are, that is all they have. Treat any correspondence with these folks like a real interview. And, no matter what, say "please" and "thank you." In fact, go out and stock up on a box of thank you notes or get in the practice of sending gratitude letters. It's all about the exchange of energy and the last thing you want to signal is an "all-take" user personality. Be grateful, be graceful, be kind. If you feel someone has done something special or a little extra, send them a small present, like a gift card to a favorite coffee shop or quality chocolates. And remember their generosity when you've achieved your professional goal and someone reaches out to you. That is when you know you're really on your way.

"I'm going straight to the top, oh yeah. Up where the air is fresh and clean."
— Straight to the Top, Tom Waits

3.4
YOU'RE UNEMPLOYED:
5 STEPS TO A FRESH START

As each December companies scramble to meet budgets, lots of people lose their jobs. It's a cruel month to be let go. And yet it's when firms, focused on making their numbers, are most likely to do so.

I know too many individuals — talented, educated, proven — that had to face their families during the holidays and share the bad news. These lay off seasons aren't easy. They are frustrating. And they can be very long. Playing victim won't help.

So here's 5 steps you can take that can position you to towards professional success.

1. **"It's Not Personal. It's Business."** Yes, *The Godfather* was right. So many decisions that happen in Corporate America have nothing to do with whether people like you or even what your contribution is. Companies don't exist to hire and keep employees. Instead, these cut and dry decisions have everything to do with keeping shareholders happy.

2. **Breathe.** Losing your job may feel suffocating. Right now it's important to take the time to breathe. Get fresh air. Eat right. Work out. Sleep well. Mental and physical strength go hand in hand and you'll need every ounce of all of it as you run the job hunt marathon.

3. **Assess Your Assets.** Not just your bank account. Take stock of your skills, your accomplishments and your education and update your resume and your LinkedIn profile. You have a lot to offer to a new firm. Time to show, not tell.

41

4. Use Your Network. Whether via LinkedIn, email, phone, Facebook or even in person, each week, let at least 10 people know that you've lost your job and what kind of professional opportunity you are seeking. Keep the message simple, something your immediate network can then share with their people. Mass emails reach a wide net, but aren't as personal.

5. Give Back. Volunteer at a new non-profit. Help a friend with their resume. Donate items that someone else may need even more than you. Giving back results in two benefits: it boosts your inner worth and it introduces you to new people that can then help connect you with just the right open door.

This is also a great time to re-evaluate your professional direction. Granted, finances, timing, responsibilities and even geography may determine your risk scale. Only you can decide that.

But, as corporate leaders play chess games with their employees, as my good friend Brad Fellows likes to say, "You are the CEO of your career."

ENTRANCE →

"WHEN CONSIDERING SOMETHING NEW, LOOK FOR THE SIGNS."

#CREATIVECADENCE

#DateYourCareer.
photo: a. sukhoy

TRANSITIONS

"A change would do you good." – Sheryl Crow

"You're my mission!" – Captain America, Winter Soldier

4.1
BE THE CAPTAIN

When navigating towards your dream job, be prepared to get there in two steps or even three. Deliberately charter your course towards multiple career harbors, each steering you closer to your desired professional destination.

Be the captain, or someone else will.

"Don't call it a comeback, I've been here for years." – LL Cool J

4.2
STAY AT HOME PARENTS: STAY ACTIVE

If you're a stay at home parent and plan to return to the work force in five years or in fifteen, keep yourself professionally active:

- consulting
- part-time jobs
- online courses
- industry seminars or
- even internships

Other backgrounds/circumstances that call for the same level of (re-)integration:

- **College and Graduate School Grads** – Young adults who have to signal they're a valuable risk for a modern company
- **America's Military** – Men and women, some of whom have done battle to keep our country safe, who now need a way to package their skills as relevant in the civilian workforce
- **Recently Laid Off** – Hard-working and loyal employees that saw the writing on the wall (or didn't) and must get un-stuck from the feeling of betrayal and rediscover their self-worth
- **Company Defectors** – Leaders that are in good jobs but no longer receive the satisfaction in their roles and don't know what's next; but do know the existing reality is no longer viable

You'll thank yourself when it's time for you to apply for jobs and be measured against folks who are industry current.

"I'm always thinking about creating. My future starts when I wake up every morning... Every day I find something creative to do with my life." – Miles Davis

4.3
GUILT-FREE FUTURE

When the right opportunity arises, don't feel guilty about changing bosses, departments or even companies. An organization's only loyalty is to their shareholders.

Which means you're the one that's accountable to being loyal towards yourself.

"We all fly. Once you leave the ground, you fly. Some people fly longer than others." – Michael Jordan

4.4
LOVE IT. OR LEAVE IT.

Some say life is long. Others say life is short.

What's certain is that life offers zero guarantees.

When determining your next career move, ask yourself what you love to do AND what can pay the bills. The bigger that Venn diagram is the closer you are to your true calling.

At a time when companies offer zero loyalty to their employees, leave what no longer makes sense.

But have your back-up plan set, first. And if you absolutely must work at a job that that has nothing to do with your dreams, then at least have that paycheck fund those passions. And, of course, pay the bills.

"Ever tried. Ever failed. No matter. Try Again. Fail again. Fail better." – Samuel Beckett

4.5
MAKE IT BETTER

We live in negative times, surrounded by perpetual pessimists eager to rain on everyone's parade.

Because they don't see a way out.

But you do.

If you don't like your school, job, company, career, business or geography, decide what you want, develop a plan and every single day work towards achieving your goal.

It is in you to make it better.

"Every exit is an entry somewhere else." – *Tom Stoppard*

4.6
HAVE GOOD EXIT STRATEGY

One of the biggest frustrations I hear from so many clients who want to get to the next step is that they don't really know what they want to do, they just know that their current work no longer satisfies them. Reasons you've shared with me include:

- Bad chemistry with a new boss

- The company culture changed, and not in a way that aligns with your own values

- You don't feel valued and respected for the work you do

- You've outgrown the job, feel bored and understand there's no growth opportunity

- The city where you live just doesn't feel like home anymore

As you think about your future, have a plan.

Because sometimes the best move ahead is a good exit strategy.

"KEEP YOUR RESUME CURRENT. ALWAYS BE READY FOR THE RIGHT OPENING."

- CREATIVECADENCE

#DateYourCareer.
photo: a. sukhoy

RESUME EXCELLENCE

"So you, with that impressive résumé and the big speech about your so-called work ethic-
I, um- I thought you would be different."
– Meryl Streep, The Devil Wears Prada

"I coulda had class. I coulda been a contender. I coulda been somebody."
— Marlon Brando, On the Waterfront

5.1
BE A STAR

Your Resume isn't your job review.

Firms aren't incented to give you favorable feedback, regardless of your performance, because there's a limited allocation of funds correlating to each department and division within the firm.

Shareholders getting their due is the priority. Not you.

So when you write your Resume be confident in your accomplishments.

Be a star.

"I'm building it brick by brick." – Iggy Pop

5.2
BUILD YOUR RESUME

You've established your platform and equipped your career toolbox. Now comes one of the most important steps in your professional journey: building your Resume. The sheer thought of this document terrifies many as no one knows where to begin. Or, you may have an existing resume, but one that's been around longer than the last presidential administration. Either way, you're looking to position yourself as the success you are and, with very minor exception, resumes are your foot in the door. So take the time to invest in this 4-step exercise to develop the best one to two page representation of your skill set.

- **Success** - While it's important to be humble in life, during the job hunt, especially in a competitive marketplace, you need to project confidence, strength and accomplishment. When you start making your list of things you've done in your past positions, skip the job descriptions and go right for the quantifiable achievements. Ask yourself this question: How did I make a difference in this role? Differentiate yourself.

- **Action** - The general rule of thumb is don't repeat verbs and, if you have to, don't repeat within the same job and definitely never in the same bullet point. Invest in a thesaurus, paper or on-line, and start looking up action verbs that best articulate your accomplishments throughout your professional history. Everyone's managing and developing something or someone. Show people what you actually do.

- **Brevity** - One of the biggest mistakes people make on their resumes is including their entire life history, thus turning a document that will be skimmed by someone within 30 seconds of time into War and Peace. Think of a film trailer you recently watched in a theater, a trailer that got you so excited that you had to go and spend your hard earned money on a movie ticket. That is exactly what your resume needs to be: a highlight of your best stuff. Once it lands in the right hands and people invite you for an interview, that's when you get to share your story.

- **Perfection** - Life is not perfect. But your Resume needs to be. This means everything's spelled correctly, formatted consistently and reflected accurately. No typos. No errors. No mistakes. While we are all human creatures, we're also signal readers, and a hiring manager, whether an academic director, corporate recruiter or even the start-up owner who makes his own copies and saves every paperclip, will often dismiss candidates whose resumes aren't perfect. Their thought is "If this person doesn't pay attention to detail with their own work, how can I possibly trust them with mine?" First impressions count.

Finally, take a good look at your Resume.

And ask yourself this question "Would I hire myself?"

Your answer will tell you if you're on track.

"It's not about the awards. If it's good, I'll do it." – *Adrian Grenier, Entourage*

5.3
YOUR RESUME
THE FILM TRAILER OF YOUR CAREER

When I was starting in this business Kim Ruggeri, a Cleveland State University, Monte Ahuja School of Business lecturer invited me to come speak to her marketing students about the industry, Corporate America and jobs. This was 2010 and the economy was still sketchy.

I really wanted to connect with the students and thought about how to best frame the expectations of their jobs search. A film lover since childhood, this eureka moment happened the morning of: **That is exactly what your resume needs to be: the movie trailer of your career.**

And in that very moment, I knew I had them.

I could see it in their eyes: they made the connection between something abstract and vanilla to something tangible and exciting. Suddenly, the idea of the resume was no longer this begrudging, laborious chore. It had, in that split second, transformed into a sexy, visible and desirable goal.

Who doesn't want their life to be a trailer, for global audiences to see?

I have since shared this analogy with my career coaching clients, film and business students and industry experts on both sides of the fence. This now endorsed realization has gotten me to think deeper. Surely, the metaphor between a good film trailer and a good resume doesn't stop there.

- **Know Your Logline!** - In Hollywood, when pitching a script, you're expected to know your logline. This is the one key sentence that tells perspective producers what the film is about: Many script investments have happened solely because of the logline. The positioning statement at the top of the resume is exactly the same thing. Hiring managers will give your file only six seconds of their time. What makes you memorable?

- **What's Your Star Power?** - A movie draw often depends on, "Who is the star?" Names and brands signal a certain reputation. You will get people excited if you've done well with companies are globally recognized industry game-changers.

- **Play to Your Audience!** - When you do go see a movie at a multiplex, the film trailers are all meticulously researched and segmented to the genre and audience of the feature. Your Resume distribution strategy should not be any different. Do the research and see what aligns. Apply where you'll fit in.

"It's like in chess: First, you strategically position your pieces and when the timing is right you strike."
— Jeff Goldblum, Independence Day

5.4
12 DAYS OF RESUMES

It's easy to get overwhelmed during the job search process. It's also easy to lose one's sense of self.

As you plan out your strategy, I challenge you to really make time for yourself, especially when it comes to your career. Don't attempt to do all in one day. Just block out 20 – 30 minutes a day and make yourself your priority.

- **Day 1: Print.** As in go into your computer, find your most recent resume version and print it out. Next, shut off the Internet, the phone and any other distractions and read the document out loud. Does it reflect your most current you? Or an older version of someone you once were professionally?

- **Day 2: Reflect.** What have you accomplished over the past year? You may be tempted to reference your annual job review, though those tend to be far more subjective and negative as they are by design not in your fiscal favor but in the shareholders'. Instead ask: How much did you make a company? How much did you save? What kind of clients did you secure? Did you get a promotion? Start adding these distinctions.

- **Day 3: Prune.** Now that you've added things, what are you going to remove? Perhaps some of the older positions — or older accomplishments — no longer hold water to the successful employee you are today? Only you can decide.

- **Day 4. Volunteer.** Maybe you're already volunteering. Take all the community work you do and add it to the bottom of your resume so that you can signal a life outside the office. Don't be afraid to add interests. These can be valuable talking points during your interview.

- **Day 5. Format.** While the standard resume still holds true, there's some wiggle room when it comes to font and layout. No matter what you do, be sure that it's easy to read and that all the same information (companies job titles, locations, dates) can be found in the same place and treated the same way, position to position.

- **Day 6. Socialize.** Your resume can't live in a vacuum. Whether you're job hunting or not, be sure to update your LinkedIn profile, incorporating the highlights and key information. Be careful with hard numbers, though. LinkedIn is public and some company info is confidential. It's acceptable to share to some of the figures on your physical resume, but it's best to be a bit more general on social media.

- **Day 7. Upload.** Get your resume live on the various career sites. This will help those sites collect and post the best opportunities for you. Select the best privacy options for you. Most sites will allow you to upload with your name and contact info to remain private, which is important for security issues, not to mention if you're currently employed.

- **Day 8. Share.** There's a good chance you've had recruiters contact you. Check your inbox and contacts and drop them each a personal, quick message. Let them know that this is your current resume and if something specific of interest comes their way to keep you in mind. This makes their job easy and, most likely, you'll be the first person they think of when the right opportunity appears.

- **Day 9. Risk.** Apply for a job that you don't think you're qualified for. You never know what happens. Also, companies keep electronic resumes on file for a certain specified time period. Perhaps you don't get that dream job but, down the line, the firm may contact you regarding another position that you are perfectly suited for and, eventually, get.

- **Day 10. Review.** Ask someone you trust to review your Resume. Be sure to respect their schedule and understand that you may have to pay them for their expertise. Give them permission to be honest. You may not like what they have to say. The good news is that you can take all or nothing of their feedback. However, know this: there's always room for improvement and an objective professional may give you that one piece of goodness that will take your document to the next level.

- **Day 11. Schedule.** Whatever calendar program you use, be sure to schedule quarterly reviews of your resume and stick to those dates. If you don't put yourself first, the rest of the world will put you last.

- **Day 12. Save.** Save that document in multiple places. Whether you have a back up system or not, find several ways to save it off your hard drive so that if anything happens, you can easily retrieve it. One easy way to do this is to email it to yourself.

There you go. Now you can kick off your job search in professional style, ready for wonderful opportunities to come your way. And, if you're still feeling even mildly guilty about giving yourself the attention that you deserve, realize that when that promotion or new job does become part of your reality, it will positively impact those who already love you anyway.

"They wanna get my gold on the ceiling," – The Black Keys

5.5
5 WAYS TO SPRING CLEAN YOUR RESUME:
LET YOUR GOLD SPARKLE

Overhauling my own Resume taught me to be even more compassionate and patient when working with my clients. It also helped me evolve it to the next level, reaching the overworked, understaffed and underpaid decision-maker audience even quicker. Below is a list of things I learned along the way that will help you to let go and move on.

1. **Transience.** In our world of texts and key words, there's always a way to say something faster. Leave out transitional statements and even the how or why of what you accomplished and just state the what. Keep each accomplishment to 1 - 2 lines. Give them the rest in the interview chair.

2. **Test.** "How was what you did in that one job relevant to what you want to do now?" asked my marketing friend. Great question. One specific company no longer reflects my current goals. So I removed it entirely. (Left as one-liner on LinkedIn.)

3. **Truncation.** One corporation where I worked for 4+ years was taking up nearly half a page. This was costing too much resume real estate space. So I collapsed all the roles into one working title and just highlighted the most relevant accomplishments of my tenure with the firm.

4. **Theme.** Because I've worked in multiple industries, and continue to do so, instead of keeping things linear I organized my positions by industry category: Academia, Business, Publishing/Writing. This immediately gives the reader precise flow, aligning similar roles within the various sections.

5. **Truth.** Yes, of course you MUST be honest on your resume. There are very easy ways to check on this today. And weather the resume, LinkedIn or an online application, consistency matters.

The past is just that. To be in demand today, it's critical to understand how one fits in with today's market needs. And express those goals quickly, clearly and confidently. So go ahead and polish your resume gold. You never know who will take notice of your brilliance.

"Short everything that man has touched." – Steve Carell, The Big Short

5.6
5 REASONS WHY BREVITY MATTERS

A friend of mine interviewed a candidate who showed up with a 12-page resume. Bad idea!

I get lots of questions on how long a resume should be and shouldn't be. Here's what I tell my clients and students: give yourself a page for each decade of experience. Of course there are exceptions, especially if you've built yourself a nice media platform, but unless there's something magical about you, keep it short. Here's why:

1. **Managers Don't Have the Time.** It's not because they're bad people or because they don't care. It's because corporations answer to shareholders. Which means companies keep staff lean. Which means that when that under-staffed and over-worked manager is taking the time to interview you, she's also missing three other meetings on her calendar. Help her find your gold.

2. **Smart Managers Smell B.S.** If you're padding your resume with accomplishments you didn't truly achieve, in today's high-network world, one phone call or social media post will refute all the pretty language you thought will help you get hired. Besides. Unless you're David Geffen, chances are you won't be able to fake your way too long. So show what you know. That's it.

3. **Signal the What. Get Invited for the How.** The verbose resumes that go on and on and on about all the ways a candidate reached a certain milestone — what I call the War & Peace approach — give the firm zero reason to invite you in for the actual interview. Don't be the boring narcissist. Instead, tease people with your impressive (and clear!) credentials. Then share your stories once you're in front of them.

4. **Presentation is Everything.** Regardless of industry, getting up in front of hiring managers, investors, key executives and other very busy people is the difference between professional growth and cubicle world. Being able to sell your ideas or yourself, quickly and effectively, is critical. So show people upfront that you can do so without taking up too much paper space or too much of their valuable time. It'll signal confidence.

5. **Got you there in 4.**

"Shine on you crazy diamond." – Pink Floyd

5.7
RESUMES: WHY LOOKS MATTER
4 WAYS TO MAKE YOUR ACCOMPLISHMENTS TO SHINE

Resumes evolve. During this decade, there's been an emergence of more creative resumes, with big bold logos, candidates' headshots and even public testimonials all on the document. Visual culture is driving this visual evolution.

At the same time, most organizations and their conservative HR departments are trained in looking at traditional resumes: typically a 2-page PDF file that showcases who you are, what you've accomplished and where you went to school. However, the way someone's career history is presented has certainly changed.

Most of that is the direct result of cost-cutting measures at firms that have flattened their work force. Hiring managers have the time from their office printer to the HR conference room to scan a resume. They are double-, triple- and even quadruple-booked in meetings and no longer have the support staff they once did. Your job is to make their job of knowing who you are as easy as possible.

1. **White Space.** Give the eyes and the mind an opportunity to process everything. Leave a nice 1″ margin on all four sides. And don't shrink your font to do so!

2. **Font.** Yes, drop the Times New Roman or any serif font for that matter, and instead use a clean, modern alternative like Helvetica, everyone's favorite. If you don't have that on your computer, use Arial, which I personally consider the poor man's Helvetica. It's close, but not quite the same impact.

3. **Categories.** Resume categories should be very easy to spot for the reader. Give them their proper hierarchy. If you're using 10-point font throughout your resume, then your category headers should be 12 point, all-caps and in bold.

4. **Header.** Put all your contact info into the header so that it repeats on each cascading page. Include your LinkedIn url. Drop the words "email" and "cell." At this stage, we can all recognize an email address and who doesn't have a cell phone?

"It's too much information for me." – Duran Duran

5.8
RESUMES: WORKSHEET
WHAT INFORMATION TO INCLUDE

These next 2 pages will walk you thru on how to format your Resume as well as what to include. Fill in the prompts below and then take it to a Word doc. Keep to 1 page per 10 years of relevant work experience.

Header: Your contact info, including your LinkedIn URL: linkedin.com/in/alexsandrasukhoy/ Skip words like "email" and "cell number."

Your 2 - 3 line positioning statement. Include who are you and what you bring to the table. Skip what you're looking for. No one cares. They care about what they're looking for.

EXECUTIVE SUMMARY – Think of this as The Greatest Hits of Your Career
- **Industry Accomplishment** – Something quantifiable and amazing you achieved; add $, % or #; skip anything that reads like a job description

----

- **Industry Accomplishment** – Something else that's quantifiable and amazing that you achieved; add $, % or #

  _____

  _____

- **Industry Accomplishment** – Yet something else and now you get to name drop big brands, big clients and big partners

  _____

  _____

- **Organizational Skill** – What's a way you play nicely with others? If you say Leadership, show how you lead

  _____

  _____

- **Organizational Skill** – What's another way you play nicely with others? If you say Communication, show what you've communicated and to what audiences

  _____

  _____

PROFESSIONAL EXPERIENCE – Repeat prompts for each relevant job

Firm Name, Firm Description City, PR/ST   **Year – Present**
Your Title

_____

- Quantifiable accomplishment; show $s, %s or #s (list from biggest impact to smallest)

  _____

- Quantifiable accomplishment; show $s, %s or #s (name drop brands, clients, partners)

  _____

- Quantifiable accomplishment; show $s, %s or #s (add awards that org, team or products won)

- Quantifiable accomplishment; show $s, %s or #s

Firm Name, Firm Description City, PR/ST   **Year – Present**
Your Title

- Quantifiable accomplishment; show $s, %s or #s (list from biggest impact to smallest)

- Quantifiable accomplishment; show $s, %s or #s (name drop brands, clients, partners)

- Quantifiable accomplishment; show $s, %s or #s (add awards that org, team or products won)

- Quantifiable accomplishment; show $s, %s or #s

EDUCATION
University, City, PR/ST

Degree, Concentration

COMMUNITY & INTEGRITY

• Community Organization, Your Title / Involvement   Year – Present

---

• Community Organization, Your Title / Involvement   Year – Year

---

"*Once you've accepted a job offer, you've also hired your next boss. Interview them first. Then make your decision.*"

#MarchForward

#CREATIVECADENCE

STRATEGY. MARKETING. COACHING.

DO YOUR HOMEWORK

"You see me I be work, work, work, work, work, work" - Rihanna

"And in this hard life I've had to navigate through"
— The Thievery Corporation

6.1
INDUSTRY AND COMPANY RESEARCH
4 WAYS TO NAVIGATE YOUR OPTIONS

Your Resume is fantastic, and now you're ready to discover your best corporate culture, i.e. your professional home. Finding that place where you can add value from day one and where your skill set will develop over time is a tricky balance, but is a very attainable goal. Laser focus, combined with flexibility, will deliver long-term mutual benefits to you and to your work. Keeping in mind a few details will help you in your journey.

1. **Be Organized** - Whether you're a journal keeper, an Excel loyalist or someone in between, index all your research information in one thorough entity. Regardless of your preferred documentation method, include the following list: organization name, address, website, phone number, social media links, account user name/password; point of contact (at least one); date you reached out, applied for job or submitted resume; next steps; misc – anything else that will help you, such as organization news, product launches, etc. No matter whom you reach out to, make sure this document chronicles your entire process.

2. **Be Open** - If you're an accountant, you can either join an accounting firm or work for any organization that requires accounting services. This is the difference between applying into an industry versus into a functional area. Each direction offers its own cost-benefit, and you can draw up your own comparison based on your career goals for the next two to three years. This same trade-off applies for the team size. In a larger organization you will likely have less influence, but will have exposure to numerous resources. In a start-up, you'll have greater influence, but within a smaller scope. Either way, everyone's lean these days, so regardless of where you'll work, you will need to take on more than you're currently trained to do. Finally, only you can decide on your future geography, but know this: the people who really love you want you to succeed, even if it means that success is in another city, state or even country.

3. **Be Passionate** - When deciding where to apply, I challenge you to bypass the common job search engines and, instead, take a look around your home: What car do you drive? Whose coffee do you drink? What magazines do you read? What non-profits receive your hard-earned money? What products or services are parts of your daily rituals? You're already a brand ambassador, so think how genuine your job interview will be when the hiring manager asks why you're applying in that specific firm or agency. In this complex market, holding education and skill set constant, your passion is the one thing that may differentiate you from your competition. Oh, and with persistence and passion, you can do what you love.

4. **Be Aggressive** - Think of your job search as a hunt, because that is exactly what it is. When six or sixty candidates are applying for the one dream position, you need to exceed your own expectation. My advice to clients is as follows: In Week 1, apply to 3 new positions. During Week 2, apply to 3 more and follow up on the first 3. In Week 3, apply to 3 additional opportunities and reach out to the first 6, etc. In your first month, you'll make progress with 12 applications. By end of Month 2, you would have reached out to 24 distinct leads. Your hunt is a numbers game. And, while you can't control whose interest you generate, you can move the odds in your favor by carrying out a full-blown campaign. Also, maximize exposure on all the major social networking sites and join any local clubs that attract other accomplished people, regardless of trade. Position yourself as the success you already are, or want to be, and watch how the world responds to you.

"You become an employee of this firm, you will make your first million within three years. I'm gonna repeat that - you will make a million dollars." – Ben Affleck, Boiler Room

6.2
WILL YOU LEAD?

If you want to see your leadership potential at an organization, take a look at the highest level positions that employees who look like you hold.

You won't grow beyond them.

And if no one in the boardroom resembles you - in terms of gender, race or even DNA - then you have your answer.

"We're gonna try something a little different this year." – Orlando Jones, Drumline

6.3
COVER LETTERS:
4 WAYS TO ATTRACT ATTENTION

You have a fabulous resume and your list of targeted firms. Your goal now is to reach out to these companies and convince them why you're the best candidate for the position. The process of selecting to whom your letters will go, the letter content and tone and the method itself is not an exact science, but, rather, a reflection of the company's culture and your own personality. Respecting hiring managers' ever eroding time, keep it short and compelling. So before you start drafting your pleas for employment, you may want to consider the following advice.

1. **Write Succinctly** – As with resumes, people don't have a lot of time to read anything, and, yet, proper protocol must be followed. As a general guideline, have one powerful introductory statement and, if there's a mutual contact or connection, be sure to include that in the very first sentence. Then, write one to two high-impact paragraphs addressing why you are the best candidate for this job, because you understand the company's needs and, based on your record, will succeed in helping the firm achieve its goals. Finish the letter with a thank you and, taking a clue from Alec Baldwin, "Always be closing." State when you will follow up with the firm and be sure to do so.

2. **Write to Your Audience** – The best advice a friend once told me when applying to an overseas college program was, "Think about the person who will read your application. Imagine what she looks like, the room she's sitting in, the time of day she will be reading your letter." This wisdom helped me get into a certain state of mind and, while I didn't fly to Paris that summer due to budgetary constraints, the program did accept me. The point being is, if you're applying at Apple, imagine the creative influence and sophisticated minimalism of that corporation. What about you reflects that same kind of progressive attitude? If your goal is a position at a law firm, is it in you to retain a level of conservatism that's expected in that industry? And, if working with kids is your dream, do you have the patience and selflessness to succeed in a school, often a very political environment? Regardless of your desired professional objective, make sure your letter reflects the consistency of a similar tone between you and the place you desire to work and provide examples that demonstrate this overlap.

3. **Write to the Job** — If you want to differentiate yourself from the hundreds of applicants competing for the same job, do yourself a big favor and read the job description. Then, if your skills match, go ahead and lift the most relevant key words and phrases and incorporate them into your letter (being careful with font consistency if you're copying/ pasting). If the job requires certain certification (CPA), a process familiarity (Six Sigma) or foreign language skills (Spanish) and you have any of them, state this! The cover letter is, ultimately a proposal: you are wooing the organization. Take it further and count the number of "I"s you have in your letter. If it's more than five, then you're focusing too much on yourself and not enough on the company.

4. **Write to the Firm's Passions, and to Yours** — Has the company recently been in the news? Has it secured a new patent? Did it sponsor a major sporting event? Is it contributing to rebuilding a community? Did it just open a new store within your driving distance? Make sure you study the firm's site, your local media and, if publically traded, any news from the Street. Gathering information today is simpler than ever and it's your responsibility to know everything you possibly can about the organization, not just for the cover letter, but also for the interview and for the job itself. Based on all you discover, marry what's key to the firm to what's key for you. If inspired, take a chance and write to a CEO whom you genuinely admire, tell her so and why you want to work for her. The more genuine your story is, the greater the likelihood of you securing your professional position.

"'Cause I am a champion, and you're gonna hear me roar!" – Katy Perry

6.4 THE INTERVIEW DECATHLON
GET TOUGH

There's a new direction in job interviews. While in the past couple of decades we could leave the interviewee chair feeling confident that we secured the position and typically did, today the approach has evolved into a complex and unpredictable multi-stage audition process.

Truth is key decision makers, in their quest to find the perfect candidate, may appear flaky in their communication. What may have once been a signal of a pending offer – even when someone verbally tells you that you have the job – no longer is. The stories I hear from my clients, students and friends continue to surprise me and, ultimately, force an ever-changing coaching approach.

If you're considering throwing yourself into the interview arena, know this: you will undergo an endurance test like no other.

What to Anticipate

- The interview process will be a long marathon followed by multiple rounds of new challenges and events. It may take several months and that's with just one organization.

- In addition to Resume, Cover Letter and Reference submissions, you will also be asked to do work for free and sans credit. This may include preparing and submitting a company strategic plan.

- Beyond phone, Skype and in-person interviews, you may also be required to travel to other cities or states and present to C-Level executives or even to the board.

- You may be given a writing assignment, a mathematical test or an exam equivalent to the GRE or GMAT to assess your written or analytical skills.

- You'll be asked to take a psychological profile/personality evaluation to see just how well you truly fit within the organization and what kind of leadership potential you have.

- This isn't some sort of trend. It's the new normal and it's occurring across multiple industries, all over the country. And the higher the position and salary? The steeper the mountain to climb.

- If a company is dictating requests and behaviors to you that cross the line of what you think is appropriate, then stop the process, thank them and move on. It's a sign of things to come.

What Does This Mean For You?

- You must be physically healthy and mentally tough. Work out regularly, eat well, take your vitamins and get solid sleep. You will need every ounce of energy you can muster.

- You mustn't exert any post-interview emotion. Whether you did fantastic or awful, only the person behind the other side of the chair makes the call. Let go, move on and curb your enthusiasm till the right, written offer lands in your lap. Channel your inner Buddha.

- No matter how excited and passionate you are about a firm, the company is looking out for its best interest and so must you. Continue to apply to other jobs and have the targeted numbers game work in your favor. At this stage it's all about options, on both sides of the table.

- Give yourself breaks to clear the mind and set up a reward system for each goal met. Applied to five key positions within one week? An extra hour of Netflix!

No matter what you do, know this: You are the only champion of your career.

"No! No exceptions! I want this job, I need it, I can do it. Everywhere I've been today there's always been something wrong, too young, too old, too short, too tall. Whatever the exception is, I can fix it. I can be older, I can be taller, I can be anything." – Michael J. Fox, The Secret of My Succe$s

6.5
YOUR JOB INTERVIEW
TIME TO SHINE

You've just received the most critical and promising news of your job hunt: an invitation to interview with one of the companies where you applied. The first interview, whether by phone or in-person, is like a first date, so impression is everything. Human resource and hiring managers know you are going to be nervous. But, you can also surprise them by presenting yourself as the confident, knowledgeable and passionate professional you are. Shining at your interview is all about preparation.

- **Investigate** – Research the company and its competition: websites, news stories, retail stores, economic trends, product launches, community work, international presence, etc. See if you have any bridged LinkedIn connections. Talk to people who are familiar with the internal culture. Companies look for fit and that is often what weeds out skilled candidates vs. retained employees. If applicable, check the stock trend and, most of all, understand the industry: markets never rest so is this a market space that will be viable in three years or is it on its way out? Finally, determine if this environment is a place where growth is possible. If the people in charge have been so for twenty years and plan on leading for the next twenty, the ceiling will be tough to break-though. Remember, this is your time and your life.

- **Invest** – Corporate attire has devolved into exaggerated casualness. But interviewing attire has retained a high standard. So, unless you're applying to a high tech start-up, wear a good suit. Different surroundings drive varying levels of conservatism. Don't fight the system. Instead, do what you have to do to get the job, and then adjust accordingly. Purchase the best quality clothes your budget affords you. If selecting existing attire, take everything to the dry cleaner. Get your shoes shined. Women, make a hair and manicure appointment and choose complimentary jewelry. Have a professional portfolio that will contain printed copies of your resume. If the interview is long distance, you may be challenged with providing your own transportation. The good news is that most interviewing expenses can be deducted at tax time. (Consult with your accountant.)

- **Include** – Once you know the date, place and time of your interview, if driving, gather directions. You may even want to drive there in prior, to find the building, entrance, etc. Determine the amount of time your trip will take in traffic, to arrive 20 minutes in advance. Waiting in your car is better than being 15 minutes late. Plus, it's customary to be present 10 minutes prior to the scheduled interview. The day of, eat something mild so your stomach isn't growling. Check yourself in the mirror one last time before heading out for the day. Take the suit jacket off and hang it in the car. Bring with you the portfolio with your resume, a notepad, pen and list of prioritized questions. If in summer, turn the air on so that you are not perspiring. Turn off your cell phone and radio and use the drive time to rehearse your opener as well as answers to anticipated inquiries. Have some emergency cash on hand in case you need to pay for parking. And, give yourself whatever pep talk works for you so that the confidence projects itself.

- **Intend** – As soon as you set foot inside, it's show time! Your interview may be with one person, or five, individually or in a panel format. Be ready for any situation and stay cool and calm. Maintain eye contact. Shake hands firmly. Don't sit down until the person conducting the interview suggests so. If asked, accept water. Your voice may need it. Listen carefully. Answer questions directly and keep result-driven stories brief. If you need extra time to reply, ask to have the question repeated and think outside the box. Look for office clues like family pictures or sports memorabilia. You may find a mutual interest that can break the nervousness. When it's your turn to ask questions, politely ask how much time the manager has so that you can focus on the most important items you need answers to in order to make a decision about your future. Finally, when the interview is wrapping up, inquire regarding next steps and, most importantly, ask for the job!

- **Invest, Again** – Within 24 hours after the interview, send personalized thank you emails to every individual who was part of your interviewing process, including the administrative assistant that did the scheduling and introductions. He is the executive's gatekeeper and needs to be respected. Your choice of communication varies and is best determined by the company and by who you are. Make sure you send one per individual (vs. one message to everyone you met) and make it personal by recalling a detail from that specific meeting. Finally, use spell check. Everything is about the impression you make, so show why you truly are the best candidate for the position.

"Let's aim high" – John Legend

6.6
AIM. FIRE.

When targeting your dream company, aim with the focus and precision of a master marksman.

Determine just how much you want to work there and then apply a full-force military campaign, strategically surprising the key decision makers that you want as your next boss.

Show them why you should be their next hiring recruit.

"Don't hate the player, hate the game" — Ice-T

6.7
PLAY THE GAME

Hiring managers interview, recruit and train from the very best they can find and are willing to pay for.

They don't stop at one perspective candidate before they commit and hire.

And neither should you.

Apply to and screen as many targeted companies as possible, realizing that, in the end, it's about the numbers.

Your job is to be the player.

And to play the game.

"Give it away give it away give it away give it away now
I can't tell if I'm a kingpin or a pauper" – *Red Hot Chili Peppers*

6.8
DON'T GIVE IT AWAY

Extracting your ideas & giving you lots of company related homework is the new job interview normal.

Be careful as to not let your enthusiasm for the position translate into you giving away your intelligence for free during the process.

At the end, the offer - with high probability - will be given to the lowest bidder or the internal candidate who, lacking your skills, knows the process.

And now, your ideas.

"It's called gratitude, and that's right" — Beastie Boys

6.9
SAY THANK YOU. AND CONNECT.

When you interview with any organization, immediately connect with every single person that took the time to meet with you - HR, hiring manager, secretary, etc.

Send them a personal and brief Thank You note as well as a LinkedIn connection request.

This way, whether you get the job or not, you've just opened yourself a new door.

DATE YOUR CAREER

"Today's companies don't measure your loyalty by your tenure. They measure it by your consistent delivery of profits."

#MarchForward

#CREATIVECADENCE
STRATEGY. MARKETING. COACHING.

ON THE JOB

"We were always told we could be anything, do anything." – Anne Hathaway, The Intern

"People still think of me as a cartoonist, but the only thing I lift a pen or pencil for these days is to sign a contract, a check, or an autograph." – Walt Disney

7.1
YOU'RE A CONTRACT

You're a Contract

Your boss is not your friend.

HR is not your friend.

The CEO is not your friend.

You are there to serve out a mutually agreed upon commitment: You provide a certain service. In exchange the company pays you. Beyond this weekly or monthly transaction, don't for one minute assume that friendship is part of the deal.

You're a contract.

"Zip it!" – Mike Myers, (Dr.Evil) Austin Powers

7.2
KEEP YOUR MOUTH SHUT!

Your first 30 days on the job, keep your mouth shut.

Of course, you should work hard and network. Obviously, meet or even exceed deadlines.

However, if you're seeking long-term success, that first month, act the observer. Feel the heat of the organization: Who has the power? What do they say at meetings? How do they behave and dress? Take note.

Then slowly, methodically and deliberately begin the conversation, assimilating and aligning with those who run the show.

"Nothing behind me, everything ahead of me, as is ever so on the road."
— *Jack Kerouac, On the Road*

7.3
YOUR FIRST 3 MONTHS ON THE JOB.
BUILDING A ROADMAP FOR THE FUTURE.

Congratulations!

After all that hard work, focus and dedication, you are starting your new job. A major accomplishment that calls for a celebration, as you enter the professional organization, be sure to put your best foot forward, right from the beginning.

Realize that navigating and absorbing the corporate culture will determine your success rate often even more so than the specific skills sets you're currently employed to demonstrate. You're on stage, watched and observed by everyone from the administrative assistant all the way to the CEO, so make sure you are truly ready.

- **Learn**. Acquaint yourself with your immediate and extended team, so, unless handled for you, initiate the conversations yourself: ask people for a morning cup of coffee, a lunch or even, once within a comfort level, a post-work drink and/or activity. Know this is a chess game and, as much as you are learning what the individuals' positions are (hierarchies are everywhere), they are also sizing you up, determining your strengths and weaknesses.

- **Leverage**. Once you have a good feel for the people and for the projects at hand, determine how you can make an immediate impact in what is, most likely, a very lean structure. Assess the problems at hand, the assets the firm has and your own talents, then, combining optimism and genuine passion, always keeping you boss in the loop, go for it. Not only will you begin to generate a positive buzz within the company, but you can also start tracking your list of accomplishments, which become critical during job review and promotion time. Most importantly, you will indicate your commitment to the firm.

- **Lead**. Regardless of your title, position or job description, everyone has the opportunity to lead. Again, make sure you notify your boss and, before taking time on her already stretched schedule, flesh out the big vision and the details, including timing, funds and manpower, as well as desired outcome, such as fiscal growth, process improvement or a fantastic new product idea. Finally, no matter what you do, stand clear of, yet never underestimate, the gossip mill and the negative/toxic "this is how we've always done it" employees who may be threatened by your presence and who are well-integrated into the cultural politics.

The best managers lead by positively rallying others around them towards achieving a common and clear goal that benefits the bottom line. Be that leader and watch your career prosper.

"All men can see these tactics whereby I conquer,
but what none can see is the strategy out of which victory is evolved." — Sun Tzu

7.4
SHOW ME THE STRATEGY

One of the most bastardized expressions in Corporate America is, "We have to be more strategic."

Executives love throwing it around because it makes them sound like they're on board, when, in fact, very few of today's leaders have any idea what that statement even means.

Next time your boss or coworker tells you to be more strategic ask them what that looks like.

Then watch them spin.

"One step at a time. One punch at a time. One round at a time." – Sylvester Stallone, Creed

7.5
5 WAYS TO SET YOUR ANNUAL JOB GOALS
YOU'LL THANK YOURSELF LATER.

During the first few months of the year, corporate executives push down company goals to senior managers who, in turn, push them down on their employees. The idea is that the lower-ranking staff accomplishments roll up the hierarchy and that by the end of the year the company achieves its fiscal objectives.

Some firms have developed fantastic goal forms and processes. How do you know they're good? They're simple. As one senior executive once shared to a room full of people, "If you're working on more than three high-level projects then your bosses aren't managing you correctly."

This comment made his direct reports very nervous.

Unfortunately, most organizations, whether for profit or not have a difficult time prioritizing and focusing, instead stressing everything is urgent. This creates chaos. And, unless employees are smart on how they co-write their annual goals, twelve months from now, they'll create even more chaos.

So, before you sign off on someone else's vision of your progress, stop and think through things.

Here are five things you can do now that will help you later:

1. **Share**. Collaborate with your boss on setting your goals so that you know, up front, what is expected of you. This includes knowing what the company is trying to achieve and how you play a part.

2. **Simplify.** If your boss isn't good at knowing what's important and what isn't, delicately help him or her get there. It's a nuanced dance, so position your thoughts in a respectful manner. Listen more. Talk less.

3. **Show.** What does success look like? For you? For your department? For the company? The less words and the more objective these achievements can be stated upfront the less subjective ambiguity you'll experience come review time.

4. **Stretch**. Ask your boss for a stretch goal. Again, be specific. If it's leadership, then have you met the goal by attending a related course or by leading a team through a complex project? How will you and your boss know it has happened and within what time frame does it need to occur?

5. **Save**. Document your high-level contributions. Either on a weekly or monthly basis, keep a log of how what you're doing is rolling up to your goals. Keep this on-going list in a format that doesn't belong to the company — either on your own personal smart phone or in a journal. This will be your supporting evidence when meeting with your boss.

At the end of the year – or during the 6-month mid-year review – you will be better prepared to not just defend your contributions but, also, to prove that you met or even exceeded the bar originally set. Don't forget, firms are not incented to give you a favorable job review because divisions and departments have fixed budgets for annual raises and bonuses. But you can do your part to show up. Not just for them, but, more importantly, for yourself.

"Keep on rockin' in the free world" – Neal Young

7.6
ROCK YOUR MIDYEAR GOALS:
5 STEPS FOR THE NEXT 6 MONTHS

While some firms are disciplined to execute mid-year reviews with their employees, in most cases the bosses are too busy growing the bottom line. During the summer months, it's easy to let go of the career reigns. Yet it's this very moment that matters tremendously to what happens to your professional path in the following year. This is even more critical when you work for yourself.

The bad news? You're halfway through the year and can't change anything that's happened during the winter and spring. The good news? You can make a great impact during the summer and fall.

1. **Read.** Track down your annual goals back in January. If you work for someone, they should have been explained, upfront, by your manager. They are usually a trickle down of organization/department/you. If you are the boss, pull out the business plan you sweated over to prepare for this year.

2. **Review.** Go through the objectives. See what you've accomplished, what's been neglected, then determine the reason for the gaps. Did the company shift direction or get restructured? Did an unforeseen project fall into your hands? Whatever the reason, speak with your boss regarding signing off on the adjusted goals so that you're measured against what is vs. what was.

3. **Regroup**. How do you step up now? Will you improve your skills by taking a class or seminar? Is your marketing plan, including social media, reflecting what you want to signal about your organization? What are you communicating and to whom?

4. **Reorganize**. Do you, as a boss, have to make personnel changes so that the best people are in the right jobs? Is it time to evaluate your vendors and professional partners to see if they're still a good fit within your organization? Once those decisions are made, be sure to share them, openly, with your team, so they are clear and on board.

5. **Relaunch**. Markets never rest. And sometimes the pace of business moves quicker than we're prepared to handle. In those cases, it makes most sense to let go of past goals almost entirely because your firm now has a completely different specialty. In order to best attract the clients that will benefit from this re-branding, consider your past investments a sunk cost and move onto where the profit is. If you work for someone, and are smart enough to understand your skills aren't where the company's goals are, either reposition yourself within the organization or start looking for a new job.

"The best things in life are often waiting for you at the exit ramp of your comfort zone."
— Karen Salmansohn

7.7
Q4: RAMPING UP YOUR CAREER

During Q4 organizations race to finish a successful year. It's also the time to hone your personal business plan. During the October / November / December holiday season, organizations often pause hiring decisions as they evaluate fiscal results and strategic goals. Take advantage of this and carve out some time to incubate what will matter in your professional journey.

Questions to ask yourself:

- Am I fulfilled and positively challenged in my existing job?

- Am I getting paid my worth? Do I even know my worth?

- Am I ready to transition from where I am to the next professional opportunity?

- Is my Resume and LinkedIn profile signaling my past or my desired future?

- Can I benefit from a proven and trusted Career Coach?

"Damned and incredible straight out the gate." — Tech N9ne

7.8
BEFRIEND THE GATEKEEPERS

If you want access to key decision makers at your place of work, first and foremost befriend their gatekeepers.

The Administrative Assistants are the loyal eyes and ears of their bosses, as well as of the organization. They typically outlast other employees and know exactly what's about to happen in any given department.

Be nice to these people. As in genuinely and sincerely kind and respectful. Say Please. Say Thank You.

And don't for one second think that their work is below yours.

"I think, team first. It allows me to succeed, it allows my team to succeed." – LeBron James

7.9
PROTECT YOUR TEAM

The people who work for you are the reason you may get a bonus. While they may not.

Each direct report will require a different management style, so adjust accordingly. Communicate clearly. Set achievable goals. Provide them with actionable training. Get out of their way so that they can do what they're hired to do.

Take them to lunch. Buy them meaningful gifts. Don't ever bullsh*t them.

And if you have the guts, ask them to give you a job review.

You can always be a better boss.

"I've had to keep exploring different ways of presenting the music so I don't repeat myself." – Tori Amos

7.10
PRESENT YOURSELF. OR DISAPPEAR.

You may be the greatest researcher, analyst or writer on your team. Perhaps you have the ability to see and solve problems like no one else can.

However, unless you consistently present your findings and solutions in front of various audiences and be convincing in the room, you might as well not exist.

It is the people who can confidently sell their ideas to key decision makers that get the visibility that leads to promotions, raises and bonuses.

Everyone else might as well press the career mute button.

"Show me the money!" — Cuba Gooding Jr., Jerry McGuire

7.11
SIZE MATTERS.
AND DECIDES YOUR PAYCHECK.

Be cognizant of the department size you work for. As more firms move towards a pay-for-performance compensation model, be aware of how that impacts your pay.

There's a high probability that a Tier 3 employee in the flagship division has fiscally outperformed the Tier 2 or even Tier 1 employee in a small division. Yet the former may get no salary increase or, even worse, be put on a corrective action plan. All the while the latter, for contributing less, may get a raise and potentially a nice bonus.

Your P&L performance should drive your paycheck.

Anything less simply doesn't measure up.

"I don't follow other players or the tournaments they play.
I have my own schedule and do my own thing." – Maria Sharapova

7.12
BEWARE THE CLEAR SCHEDULE.

The days of having 3 big priorities are over. Today, most managers at most firms have multiple meetings, projects and deliverables all happening simultaneously.

Ask anyone with a significant role at an organization the last time the felt caught up.

It was probably during the Clinton Administration. As in 20 years ago.

If your schedule suddenly begins to open op - meetings not invited to, projects lifted and deliverables reassigned, get your energy level, Resume and LinkedIn profile in top shape.

Because your clear schedule leads to an empty desk.

"If you continue to work hard, let that be the fuel to your fire." — Pitbull

7.13
FIRE YOUR HIGH-SKILL EMPLOYEE

Not the one that has a great attitude. But the one with the bad attitude. That rare mix of knowing her job really, really well, but also bringing a toxic energy into the room.

You know these people, they claim to have all the work related answers and solutions, but they are negative, pushy and judgmental. They smile to your face and then gossip about you the moment you leave the room. They enjoy showing everyone how great they are at the expense of making those around them feel like crap.

These high-skilled employees may know their craft. But they are a cancer to the organization. Ultimately, no matter how much they deliver in productivity, they bring everyone else's down. And cost companies hundreds of thousands of dollars due to high turnover from those that deserve better treatment.

So let these toxic people go. It's either them or your profits.

SOCIAL NETWORKING

Friend: Why are you on Facebook all day? Don't you have a job?

Me: It's my job to be on Facebook all day.

"Fresh, fresh, fresh, yes I'm fresh." — *Remy Ma*

8.1
UPDATE YOUR LINKED FREQUENTLY

Update your LinkedIn profile on a regular and frequent basis.

Not only does this help with the search engine/key word process to attracting your next job, but it also doesn't raise a red flag to your current employer that an overnight profile overhaul will.

Companies look for 5 things on LinkedIn:

- Are you on it?

- What have you accomplished?

- Who do you know?

- What have people said about you?

- How in tune are you with your own industry?

"I'm the one fighting, okay? Not you, not you, and not you." – Mark Wahlberg, The Fighter

8.2
5 QUICK WAYS TO STRENGTHEN YOUR LINKED IN PROFILE.
BOOST YOUR PROFESSIONAL PRESENCE.

As a Career Coach, my job is to make sure that I'm aware of the changing trends within the global workplace. It's no secret that after a decade in the game, LinkedIn has evolved as the dominant professional networking site, platform to the careers of nearly 500 million job seekers, hiring managers, entrepreneurs and recruiters.

What does this mean for you? For one thing, it means you have a very powerful tool at your disposal to ensure that you are shining your accomplishments in their best light. Like all relationships it also demands responsibility and commitment.

Here's 5 simple steps you can take this week and give yourself the necessary boost:

1. **Update Your Photo** – Your LinkedIn profile photo should reflect what you look like at your day at work. If you're a C-level executive, this means you in a suit, well groomed and smiling. If you're a filmmaker, then have someone snap a sharp image of you with your camera in hand. Regardless of what you do you for a living, don't include a spouse, a dog or a baby in your headshot. None of these is professional. Save the personal for Facebook.

2. **Update Your Headline** – You are more than your job title. But your Headline currently automatically reverts to it. That does not have to be the case. Customize it to reflect a bigger and more focused picture of who you are and what you bring to an organization.

3. **Update Your Current Position** – Have you been promoted? Have you changed jobs? Do you have new responsibilities? Did you execute a long and successful project? Update this on a monthly basis while the changes are still fresh in your mind.

4. **Update Your Publications** – Depending on where you are in your career, there's a pretty good chance that the bigger you are an expert, the more publications want to know what you think about certain topics. LinkedIn now has a section for that and you can even include the URL of the media link as well as add co-authors.

5. **Update Your Company Links** – Most established firms now have a dedicated LinkedIn page. If your company thread currently shows corporate logos, you are in a good place. If not, edit the company and see if it pops up, image in hand. These logos make for a more vibrant LinkedIn resume and can often capture someone's attention quicker than reading a company name.

"The keys to brand success are self-definition, transparency, authenticity and accountability."
— Simon Mainwaring

8.3
YOUR SOCIAL MEDIA PRESENCE IS YOUR BRAND
5 COMMON SENSE REMINDERS

1. Be the same person across multiple platforms

2. Even if you hit delete anything you post on the web is there forever

3. Cultivate your own voice, perspective, POV; introduce industry relevant topics via your lens

4. Unless you're running for office, stay away from political and religious discourse

5. Give people a reason a to follow you

Convert your skills into revenue.

Photo: a sukhoy, Cleveland 2014

#MarchForward
#CREATIVECADENCE
STRATEGY. MARKETING. COACHING.

GIG ECONOMY

Self-Employed
Freelancer
Virtual Employee
Independent Contractor
Business Owner
Entrepreneur
CEO of One

"I never pictured myself as just a rapper; I always wanted to act and do whatever else I could do. I always felt like I could do a lot of different things." – Queen Latifah

9.1
STARTING YOUR OWN BIZ - PART 1
10 FIRST STEPS: WHERE TO BEGIN

So many people I know are leaving the rat race and going off on their own. Leaving the predictable structure and secure income behind isn't easy, especially when health benefits and annual bonuses can be counted on. However, given the zero-loyalty corporate game, no one's job is secure.

Today's work force is about flexibility, adaptability and risk. It's also about the hustle and multiple revenue streams.

Entrepreneurship is hard and is certainly not for everyone. I started my business when I still worked a full-time job and before the market crashed. Here's what I learned from all the uncertainty and client evolution.

1. **Think** – What kind of biz would you start? The perfect marriage is combining what you love with something you already know how to do and something the market demands. Make these into 3 independent lists, then insert them into a Venn diagram and whatever overlaps is a starting point.

2. **Check With Your Gut** – When you have your list of 1 or 4 or even a dozen things that you love and know something about, say each one out loud. If you get a funny feeling in your belly, you are probably on to something.

3. **Check With Your 6-Year-Old** – Not your kid or your niece. Check with your inner 6-year-old. What did you do, back then, when time seemed to disappear? Tap into that kid and let him speak!

4. **Trust Yourself** – Your left brain will start playing tricks on you and give you 1000 reasons why you should not be pursuing your life dream. Your fiscal responsibilities may warrant security and stability. That is for you to decide. However, chances are, if you work on something you love, others will love it, too.

5. **Commit** – You have a goal. Now channel laser focus on achieving it and being successful. And be sure to celebrate the milestones.

6. **Name It** – Brainstorm this with yourself, out loud, or with others. Hang names on a wall. Take down anything that isn't great. Sleep on it. No matter what, you've got to love the name

7. **Secure Domain** – Even if you do not have all the details worked out, securing a domain name is the first step to being first in the market with a concept. There are tons of sites to go to. Also, realize that a domain name is NOT the same as hosting. These are separate things and so are moving an existing site to a new host, creating an email address and having an interface. Make sure you have all your questions answered before purchasing a domain/hosting package.

8. **Find a Tech Person** – Unless you have been running a .com, find someone who has. Even if he charges you, you will be better off in the long run. In a perfect world, your tech guy is also your web developer. This person becomes your partner in everything and you must give him the right to object to your ideas, since he is the field expert and you are not. A great web developer should ask you a lot of questions and this will make you think more about your biz.

9. **Recruit a Creative** – This could be your web developer, a graphic designer, an artist, etc. This is the person that helps you think through the visual aspects of your site and your logo, which is your brand. So, unless you have an art or design degree, having a creative mind vs. having expertise in visual problem solving are two different things. You always want your best foot forward in a competitive market place, especially during a recession. What is going to make your look stand out in the crowd?

10. **Call your Lawyer** & **Accountant**– Have them help you set up your LLC or INC, counsel you on trademarks, copyrights, registrations, taxes, expenses, etc.

"Work smart. Get things done." – Susan Wojcicki

9.2
STARTING YOUR OWN BIZ - PART 2
10 NEXT STEPS: DAY-TO-DAY OPERATIONS

Launching your new business fuels a certain adrenaline. While opening your box of business cards is exciting, it is only the beginning of a long and intense process. The key to survival is having a plan in place and following through on it.

Being your own boss requires tremendous discipline. Having a support team? Makes all the difference.

1. **List Your A-Team** – Now that you have quality people around you, get a white board and start making a list of your A-Team. In addition to your web developer, creative person and lawyer, start drawing in others around you – the nephew who needs real experience, the parent who once opened a small business, or the best friend who always gave it to you straight. You need these people to keep you in the truth zone and support you when you're down. And, when cash is low but drive is high, you need people who believe in you.

2. **Work** – Days of the week will now blend. You may be rolling out of bed at 11am, and going to bed at 3am. But you will be working. All the time. Everywhere you go, you will notice that your conversations will ultimately lead you to discussing Your Dream. This is one of the benefits of not having to be "at the office" at 8am. But, in return, you will have to discipline yourself daily to get things done. Also, now that life's less structured, think about when you are most productive. Those will be hours the work will crank and the ideas will come. Shut everything else down during this time and get industrous.

3. **Have Weekly Coffee Hours** – No more f****** meetings. No. These are the coffee shop discussions you will be having with your A-Team on a weekly basis, sometimes one-on-one, sometimes in groups. These discussions have two benefits: they advance your business goals and they serve as great forums to give and receive moral support.

4. **Take a Day Off** – You will become obsessed on getting your biz off the ground and that is all you will breathe, think, eat and sleep. However, in order to be most productive, and not shut off people who love and need you, give yourself some time off. Also, now that 8 – 12 hours of your day will not be strangled in useless meetings, it's amazing how much more productive you will be in 3 hours of work on your own dream vs. 2 full corporate days back at the office. Your time is now your time.

5. **Get Your Biz Plan Going** – It keeps you focused, helps you prioritize and may help you secure funding. There's various online models you can download. And, if you worked in corporate, you've done this a 1000 times for someone else. Now do it for yourself.

6. **Stay Organized** – Because your days are less structured and will tend to blend, make sure you have a preferred method of organization – from appointments, to contacts to business goals, all in a format that serves you best. That includes your work space. Make sure you have a dedicated area in your home where you can focus and where you have a file cabinet, office supplies and good lighting.

7. **Network** – You may have done this for years. Now do it again, but differently. Tap into your school alumni. Get to know your neighbors. Attend related events in your city. Volunteer. Help someone with their business. Open your own doors. Read Malcolm Gladwell's The Tipping Point to get a sense for how powerful connectors are.

8. **Listen to Great Music** – Everyone has music that helps them tap into their most creative senses. Find that music and play a lot of it. Make yourself some mixes. I'll even name one for you: Songs That Make Me Want to Kick Some A**. (Listen to "The Best" by Foo Fighters and tell me it doesn't inspire you…)

9. **Take Breaks** – While an art student in undergrad, my professor used to say, "Step away from the canvas." Go jog around the block, check out the latest Snapchat feed, call a friend. Something, anything, but give your brain the rest it needs to put your best thinking into action.

10. **Invest in Technology** – Now is not the time to skimp on technology, even the basics. Invest in the right tools, the fastest at home internet connection and unlimited minutes plan.

"A dream doesn't become reality through magic; it takes sweat, determination and hard work."
— *Colin Powell*

9.3
STARTING YOUR OWN BIZ - PART 3
5 STEPS: HOW TO FUND YOUR DREAM

Before you take the crowd-fund (avoid the eye-rolling from your friends and family) or business loan (avoid the stressful application and waiting process) approaches, here's five creative ways to secure funds:

1. Keep your **full time job** and save, save, save

2. Take on a **second job** for x time or till you save x amount of funds

3. **Sell some things** that you'll be ok parting with; consider local consignment shops or online

4. Tap into **local/national orgs** that can help sponsor or finance your biz idea

5. Enter **local/national contests/competitions/fellowships** within your desired industry

"Risk isn't a word in my vocabulary. It's my very existence." – Slash

9.4
BE THE SLASHER.
AND CONVERT YOUR SKILLS INTO REVENUE.

One of the most frequent situations I encounter as a Career Coach is intelligent, accomplished and ambitious people coming to me because they feel lost. What many of you have shared with me:

- "I know how to do many things but I'm not sure which one to focus on."
- "I'm good at what I do however it doesn't reflect my passions."
- "I've been out of the workforce for a while, tending to my family, and don't know how to put my skills to good use."

The good news is two-fold. First, in today's fickle, gig economy, being good at just one thing is no longer enough. Whether you work for an organization or for yourself, the expectation is that you know how to do many things well. For example, you're an Entrepreneur/Guest Speaker/Chef/Photographer/Fund Raiser. Or you're a Doctor/MBA/Blogger/Parent/Volunteer.

In other words, you're a Slasher.

Marci Alboher first coined the term back in 2007, with her book One Person/Multiple Careers: A New Model for Work/Life Success. However it was after the market crashed in late 2008 that the workforce, coupled with accessible technology, truly began to shift in this direction.

My personal experience with this began right about that time, after exiting a 20-year career in Corporate America. What I learned is that working for yourself means you must tap into every single skill that you possess and have the simultaneous focus and flexibility to convert those skills into revenue.

What I enjoy most about being a "slasher" is that I get to meet some of the most creative and hard-work people, from every facet and geography. Even while teaching, for a couple of years it was at two different

115

colleges: at one, I taught Film Studies. At the other? Business. And when some of my clients or students say that I've made an impact, that reward alone makes it worth it.

What I like least about being a "slasher" is making small talk at business or social events when I first introduce myself and tell people what I do. I once had a man, a very successful and wealthy man, look me right in the eye and say, "There's no possible way you can be good at all of these things."

What I've learned since is to drop the "slasher" title at first meetings, introduce myself by whatever is most suitable to that specific audience and, if the relationship develops into something more long-term, then I can also share all the other professional hats I wear.

It's not just that I do all these things, it's that I am all these things.

"You'll only advance at an organization if the board looks likes you."

#MarchForward

#CREATIVECADENCE

STRATEGY. MARKETING. COACHING.

WOMEN & DIVERSITY

"If you ask men why they did a good job, they'll say, 'I'm awesome. Obviously. Why are you even asking?' If you ask women why they did a good job, what they'll say is someone helped them, they got lucky, they worked really hard." – Sheryl Sandberg

"Being short is probably as much of a handicap to corporate success as being a woman or an African American." – Malcolm Gladwell, Blink

10.1
HIGH ASPIRATIONS? HIGH HEELS!
MARCH YOUR WAY INTO CORPORATE AMERICA
JUST WEAR THE RIGHT SHOES

We live in progressive times. But our psyche is steeped in tradition.

As women graduate college at rates surpassing those of men and as white-collar office jobs continue to dwarf blue-collar manufacturing, women continue to increase our presence within the corporate arena. Simultaneously, we're still getting paid $.85 per $1.00 of our male counterparts, the same discounted rate as when I first researched the topic while at DePaul University, in 1991.

The professional options continue to increase and dress codes continue to evolve along the way. However, as recently as a decade ago while commencing my MBA at the Simon School, at the mandatory "Dress for Success" seminars, the now defunct Casual Corner reps came out to give us options. Pants? Highly discouraged, especially to women pursuing banking.

This floored me. It was 2001 and we were pressured into wearing skirt suits to interviews, not out of choice but because the banking sector expected this.

I purposely back-lashed against this devolutionary influence and, while I owned one good skirt suit and one good pant suit, I wore what felt right for the specific opportunity, based on mood, weather and what looked good that day. If I ever didn't get a job because I went against the grain, that level of feedback was never provided.

The one fashion consistency I did witness in my two decades in the corporate trenches is how much a good shoe matters. Specifically, the height and sophistication of the heel.

Because the heel adds height and height is perceived as power. And, in Corporate America, it's all about perceived power and the success this power signals.

According to the CDC, the average American man is 69.4 inches tall, while the average American woman is 63.8. In *Blink*, Malcolm Gladwell adds, "In the U.S. population, about 14.5% of all men are six feet tall or taller… Among CEOs of Fortune 500 companies, that number is 58%." Height matters. And, if you're a woman, the fight to the top looks grim.

We women, on average, are biologically shorter than men, earn less for the same job than men and have a much smaller chance of running a Fortune 500 company than men. This paints a rather skeptical present and future, but it doesn't stop women from pursuing MBAs and corporate jobs. And, for those women who are in the trenches, competing for the promotion, the new client, the bonus and the visibility to one day manage a team, earn stock options and have some stake in the game, appearance is a critical component of that game.

Heels help provide this: we feel taller, we feel noticed, we feel a new found power that washes away the second we take those pressing and expensive shoes off our tired feet after a twelve or even sixteen hour workday.

For businesswomen, beyond the suit, the right pair of heels serves as the simultaneous protective shield and lethal spear that warriors wore in Medieval times. The right heels not only give us the confidence to walk with our head held a little taller but, also, to be able to look men — those making more than us — directly in the eye, as if to say, "We are not your daughters, we are your equals."

I recall a petite female communications professor of mine telling us during one moment, when she couldn't get the attention of the room, she actually climbed on her desk. It took that extreme action for people to finally acknowledge she had something to say.

Women do have something to say, as do men, and learning to truly listen to each other and to hear one another is key, not only in a professional setting but also in a personal one. And, as many of my female friends will attest, their professions are far more conducive to comfortable shoes, where it truly is about function over form.

But, the reality today, in this schizophrenic and volatile economy, is that people want leaders who will solve problems, cut costs, recruit talent and, ultimately, deliver profits. And, as long as we think that the tall guy must be the smart one, the women have to wear their heels, one determined and painful corporate step at a time.

"It is time for parents to teach young people early on that in diversity there is beauty and there is strength." — Maya Angelou

10.2
CORPORATE DIVERSITY:
WHAT IT IS AND WHAT IT ISN'T

Lots of talk these days regarding diversity — and it's not limited to corporations. Lots of organizations, including companies, universities and non-profits, now issue diversity mission statements and even allocate dedicated teams to the cause. But how many have any idea what it means? And how is that information disseminated to everyone within that space?

If you've actually read some of these statements, you probably left more confused than before you laid your eyes on them. They are typically full of pretty words stating pretty things that make you feel warm and fuzzy. Yet, simultaneously, many say absolutely nothing and there's nothing actionable about them.

Most organizations are finally catching on that in order to best serve their customer (or end user) employees who represent the firm have to, at some level, identify with those very clients that will increase their payroll. Yes, it really does boil down to the fiscal factor. A public company's only obligations are to answer to shareholders and to be within the law. Anything else the organization wants to do is simply good PR.

Diversity is also not about quotas or affirmative action. The people who combine everything into one bucket of confusion misunderstand what diversity is. It is about alignment to the global shift and ensuring that the very best talent that represents that shift is working on your team.

How do you know if you will fit within that platform and if you have opportunity to grow? What I share every semester with my students and with many of my clients looking for new opportunities is that there is one clear way to see if you have a chance at breaking the glass ceiling within a firm vs. remaining a worker bee during your entire duration: look at the board.

If the board is a bunch of cousins, unless you're a cousin or marry into the family, you don't stand a chance. But if the board is reflective of the customer base and you resemble the clients and the key people driving all major decisions, then you have an opportunity to make an impact.

"My mom, who's been in the restaurant business for 40 years, is the number-one influence in my life. But I look up to a lot of people in the industry. Tops on my list is Mario Batali. My mom and Mario taught me the same lesson: Food is love." – Rachael Ray

10.3
MY BUSINESS INSPIRATION? MY MOM!
BY RACHEL PANKIW, M.B.A.

I hate to be writing a standard, "My Mom's been my inspiration" essay but when I sat back and really thought about who has been the constant source of wisdom and encouragement for my professional endeavors I honestly couldn't think of anyone else.

My Mom received her MBA back in the late 70s when there was a big push towards equal opportunity in the workforce. After receiving an Ivy League education, she pursued her masters from an accelerated one-year program. She had to quickly figure out how to deal with a corporate culture surrounded by male executives who were just fine keeping the status quo. She told me one story about how she initially declined a job offer as she wasn't satisfied with the proposed salary but later accepted the offer at a higher rate. She found out a year later the hiring manager had deliberately given her a lower salary offer in hopes that she wouldn't take it as he didn't want to hire a woman (but was obligated to do so by an equal opportunity mandate.)

I heard stories about her always having a pen handy after a fellow female colleague in her MBA program erased her name (written in pencil) on a sign-up sheet for a job interview. I, too, faced some of this competition when I attended a very competitive high school. I never understood those people who felt the need to put others down in order to get ahead. I strongly believe you can excel in the workforce (and in life) by advocating for your own strengths without highlighting your peers' weaknesses.

As I recently completed my own MBA program at Cleveland State University, I can honestly say I haven't faced that same intense competition my mother mentioned. My MBA program offered a variety of concentrations and there's such a broad, diverse group of students within each of those majors. We've been able to grow, struggle, and succeed without stepping on each other's toes or competing for a class rank. Perhaps it's because we all have our own interests and professional paths and are no longer tied down by the high school mentality. I have met some amazing women (and men) in my program and I can say that I am truly happy when I see them share a success story. If anything it motivates me to keep at it and it confirms to me good things come to those who work for it.

While I haven't experienced intense rivalry or inequality in my MBA program, I'd unfortunately be lying if I said that weren't the case in some of my professional endeavors. I've had the boss who micromanages and I've had the boss who doesn't act like a boss. In both scenarios, the employee is the one who gets ridiculed, not the boss. The micromanager chastised me for stepping on his toes (he wouldn't delegate-ANYTHING) and then when I stopped doing that he told me I wasn't taking the initiative or being a team player. The absentee boss knew how to make appearances look good from the outside and then when I'd politely point out the elephant in the room and inquire about possible solutions, I'd get reprimanded for not being a good employee or team player.

There are way too many bosses out there who know how to manage up (IE: keep appearances looking good with the higher ups) but not actually be a boss and manage their team (manage down.) I've had a boss ask me what I thought my performance goal should be because he couldn't think of anything and I've had another boss tell me I didn't meet a performance goal, which I didn't even know I had. I've had a boss give me an urgent project only to go play cornhole (a Cleveland pastime) for an hour in front of me and then tell me I was being a party pooper when I asked if he could keep the noise level down. My Mom has taught me how to take criticism (even if it's not valid or accurate) and smile and say "thank you for the feedback." I had a situation once where my boss told me that he didn't feel I was cutting it and perhaps he needed to lower his expectations to which I responded, "To be honest I'm not really sure what your expectations are." That response was pure art taught by my Mom. If the job gets bad enough, that's when it's time to start looking elsewhere.

The reality is job hunting is a necessary evil.

Worst case scenario you were laid off and are under the gun to find something while managing your finances, not coming across as desperate, and proving your worthiness to a new employer. Best case scenario you start looking for another job while you already have a job. I will say it is much easier to find a job when you already have a job but you still have to mentally hit bottom with your current job before you realize it's time to start looking for new opportunities. So either way job hunting is still a necessary evil.

In a way it really is like online dating. While it would be nice to just meet someone, have an instant spark, and move on with your life you need to go through those God awful first dates and send out those seemingly endless job applications. Even before you decide a relationship or a job is for you, you need to have time to let it develop. You also need something to compare it to. When you're a newbie starting out in the work force you need to take whatever you can get. I've joked with my Mom that when she graduated with her MBA, she could have majored in basket weaving and she still would have had job offers pouring in. Today's job market requires an intricate (and oftentimes unrealistic) combination of specialized skills and several years of experience just to get your foot in the door for an entry-level position. I finished my undergrad with three solid internships under my belt and I still struggled getting that first job.

I have struggled every time I was job hunting. I've found myself becoming more strategic and selective with the jobs and companies I've pursued as I've grown into my professional career (just like I've become more focused on the quality rather than the quantity of my relationships.) Unless you're mentally checked out for the week and need to hit a quota to collect unemployment, there's really no reason to submit an application to a company you wouldn't be excited to start working for the next day if you got an offer. A typical workweek involves a minimum of forty hours. You could work 8-6 and still have to read emails at night only to play catch up on the weekends. It's your mission to help fill in the gaps and make someone else's workload easier (your boss, your shareholders, etc.) Even after you get the job, there's still a major learning curve with getting up to speed and learning the nuances of the organization (not to mention where the bathroom is and what the security guard's name is.) You and the company are forming a union: make sure it's mutually beneficial before you jump in.

I'm sure everyone has had that one awful relationship you just cringe to think about now and can't help but ask yourself why you put up with what you did. To quote Oprah, "When we know better we do better."
There are things I have liked and disliked about every job (and boss!) I've had. It's important to recognize the environments you do well in and the kinds that just aren't for you. It's even more important to recognize what kind of a boss you need to have to perform your best. A lot of it unfortunately can be trial and error (especially early on) but I would definitely consider this a valuable investment. I strongly recommend taking some personality profile assessments like a Myers Briggs to get a baseline insight into the types of work environments you do well in.

My Mom has survived 17 bosses at her current job. She has told me countless stories of nepotism, pay inequality, and gender bias at different points in her career. She is at the point in her life where the pay is good, she feels she has piqued in her professional path, and doesn't feel it's worth jumping ship at this point. I'm sure she'll keep riding the wave until it's time to retire. She has done an excellent job of helping me to manage expectations as I navigate this crazy corporate world we live in.

Knowing I have someone to confide to who has been through it before and who has my back really does make a difference. I have seen it in my jobs where the young male is taken under an executive's wing to be coddled, praised, and handed countless opportunities that a female with even better credentials would have to fight twice as hard to get. I could write an entire thesis paper about the experiences I've had thus far and I'm still pretty new in my profession.

My Mom has taught me some invaluable lessons that have really helped me in my professional pursuits. I hope they help you:

- Always give credit where credit is due
- Remember to say thank you
- Handwritten Thank You notes after an interview are a must
- It doesn't hurt to take someone out to lunch or to bring in a little something as a token of appreciation for those above and beyond moments
- Go out of your way to learn everyone's names (even if they aren't in your department)

- Get friendly with the security guard, receptionist, lunch worker, etc. (they're people too!)
- I don't know the answer to that but I can get back to you is an acceptable response
- Don't be afraid to challenge the status quo if you see a valid reason to
- Stand up for yourself and your fellow females. The men have each other's backs. We need to have ours.

"My advice to women in general: Even if you're doing a nine-to-five job, treat yourself like a boss. Not arrogant, but be sure of what you want - and don't allow people to run anything for you without your knowledge." – Nicki Minaj

10.4
12 BUSINESS LESSONS MY WOMEN BOSSES TAUGHT ME

When Thomas read the first draft of this book, he came to me with a long list of feedback. Because he wanted this to a be a better tool for others and also because he knew that to push me to elevate the writing would force me to be a better writer. One of the most glaring criticisms of that first draft was that there wasn't enough of the female voice in here. Specifically, that the woman in business experience was lacking.

This was of course jarring and ironic all at once. I climbed the Corporate America ladder for 20 years and have more than earned my stripes on discussing the topic. And, simultaneously, here was a man who was telling a woman that she's not enough. Grrrr.

But, once I slept on it and thought about it and understood where Thomas, a strong advocate for women succeeding in a man's world, was trying to tell me was, "You know how it is. Now show us what it is. Because Millennials, men and women, need to know what this professional world is really like."

So I slept on it some more and the obvious fact hit me: from my first retail job while in high school thru my last corporate job post MBA, almost all my bosses were women. Furthermore, I'm still in contact with most of those women, either in real life or via social media. And I thought about what all these incredible women, who had advanced in their careers, have taught me.

I began putting together a list. Some are direct quotes. Some are overall big lessons they shared by teaching me new behaviors. Combined, this list is a good blueprint for success.

- "When business is slow, get back to basics. Keep a clean store, get your best merchandise to the front, greet every customer, demonstrate your product, smile and stay friendly. Attitude matters. And never just stand behind the register." – Andrea Pape Castellan

- "Keep yourself and your work well organized. With important events or promotional shipments, check everything twice, three times if you have to. Call ahead. Confirm. Communicate." – Marssie Mencotti

- "Go sit next to the accountant and see what problem they are trying to solve and how you can help. Go to the warehouse and pack some boxes. And don't for one second think that any one employee is more important than another. It takes everyone to run this business." – Diane Goldsher-Kornick

- "Now that you've run this product sales spreadsheet, study it and then get back to me. Tell me the story behind the numbers. What are they telling you? What are the trends? What do we do next to grow the business?" – Amy Krouse

- "Is this product sexy? Because if it's not sexy, why are you launching it?" – Monica Sanders

- "Have the most current information on your product sales and share it with everyone responsible for it, all at the same time and on a consistent basis. Address all the questions in the room. Leave everyone knowing exactly what their next steps are." – Leslie Hoadley

- "If you want to get accepted into a good MBA program, you need to show them how you've been a success and how you're going to stay a success. The schools want to know what kind of an alum you're going to be before they will invest in you." – Kendra Ensor

- "Master Excel. Know your numbers. Anticipate three different levels of management questions. And as a Product Manager, understand that your role is to facilitate every single step of the product lifecycle, from conception to sell-through. So treat all the other departments well. Listen." – Beth Murdoch

- "Organize and re-organize your team to get the job done. Pull in the right people on an important project, even if they're not the project owners, because they have talents and skills that will make it better. And don't overwork anyone." – Sally Babcock Schriner

- "How do these words sound when you put them together? Read them. Read them out loud. Read them again and again. Do they have a rhythm? Do they fill a purpose? Are they original in thought?" – Betsy Fox

- "If you want to grow your career, especially as a woman, you need to have the right mentor. And in large, important meetings, study the dynamics, then be the diplomat." – Pam Faroh Seiple

- "It's not enough to have a good idea – you must understand the marketplace. If you want your product to sell, the creative and the business decisions must work seamlessly together." – Tina Benavides

"I never paint dreams or nightmares. I paint my own reality." – Frida Kahlo

10.5
FRIDA KAHLO: MY INSPIRATION
BY BRYAN CEJA, M.B.A.

As a kid, I didn't know anything about Frida Kahlo. Hers isn't exactly the kind of art you find in schools, public places, or most museums. I first was exposed to Frida Kahlo at a lesbian bar called Little Frida's in West Hollywood when I was about 20. I was immediately drawn to the art on the walls. It was so raw, emotional, and gripping. It seemed perfect that I would find this art in a small, artsy, lesbian club cloaked in smoke tucked away amid the large gay bars of WeHo. A little gem.

I had never seen paintings like hers before. I had seen portraits before. They were usually glamorous or dignified, but Frida's self-portraits were neither glamorous or dignified. They were simply there. Looking at you the way she saw herself. She wore Mexican clothes. She had a prominent uni-brow. Her face was expressive yet also expressionless. Soft yet severe. I thought who paints themselves like this? Why would she emphasize that eyebrow? I couldn't stop staring at them. The more I looked, the more I saw. Beautiful little butterflies, leaves and a black jaguar surrounded her, like they were her friends. Her necklace had a black hummingbird on it but the necklace was made of thorns cutting into her neck. I was transfixed. There was so much to unfold here. She was complex and what seemed like a simple portrait was filled with meaning upon further contemplation. She was wounded, yet stoic. She was weak, yet strong. She was ugly (to herself), yet beautiful.

Another painting showed her as a beautiful deer romping through the woods. Yet her body was pierced by arrows, blood streaming down her body. Her face was the same; wounded yet stoic.

Frida's story is both tragic and inspiring. Her body was impaled by a metal rod in a streetcar accident. She required multiple surgeries throughout her life. She fell in love with an older man, Diego Rivera, a womanizer, and one of Mexico's greatest artists himself. His infidelity and her inability to bear children as a result of the accident only added to the pain she felt. She felt both trapped by and attracted to Diego by her circumstances and her feelings for him.

She was anything but demure though. She dove into her art. It became her career, her coping mechanism. She was pushing the boundaries of women in art. She was politically active and engaged in political activism. But it was her self-portraits that captured the world's attention, her fame growing after being "rediscovered" in the 1970's and 80's.

As I pondered the various paintings, I was amazed at her open relationship with her broken body, her looks, her pain, her fears, and her closeness with death. Everything we avoid, she embraced and made them hers. Her work exposed those feelings we all feel but are taught to hide. It exposed weakness, hurt, insecurity and awkwardness. All familiar feelings to anyone. I realized it took a strong person to flay themselves in public like that and expose the feelings that tear at our souls.

I empathized with her emotions. I shared her insecurities with how she looked to herself. I had a terrible insecurity about speaking in front of others. I felt like everyone could see my flaws, hear it in my voice. She was imperfect. I am imperfect. She was wounded. I was wounded. She was subservient to her circumstances. I am subservient to my circumstances. I don't want to be, but I am. We all are. Yet she somehow took her circumstances, her flaws, her wounds, and she made them into something beautiful.

For me, that became the lesson. Own your flaws. Own your wounds. Own your insecurities. Owning them keeps them from holding you back. It liberates you. Take them, embrace them, and use them to drive yourself to do your best while staying true to yourself.

Frida Kahlo's art had an impact on me. She allowed me to connect my Mexican identity with something cool. She helped me to channel my emotional wounds into strength. She helped me to accept who and what I was so that I could become an assertive and strong individual which helped guide my personal and professional life. I was better able to put my insecurities where they belong by confronting them and taking control of them. Giving presentations is now easy for me because I know the people I am speaking to have their own flaws and insecurities just like I do. I'm not the odd one out anymore, pretending to be perfect. I am comfortable and confident.

I am very lucky to have stumbled into that small but vibrant little West Hollywood bar in the 1980's and "discovered" Frida Kahlo purely by accident. She has become an important icon for me and an integral part of my own personal self-development. Inspiration truly comes in the most unlikely of places.

"Funny business, a woman's career. The things you drop on your way up the ladder — so you can move faster — you forget you'll need them when you go back to being a woman."
— Bette Davis, All About Eve

10.6
YOU'RE A WOMAN IN BUSINESS.
BUT ARE YOU HOT?

Lately, I've been seeing more women showing more skin on LinkedIn, finding very "stretchy" reasons to make those posts. How does posing in a bikini and writing about leadership have anything to do with leadership?

Of course these posts receive a ton of likes from men. But is that the place for it? Do women in bikinis on LinkedIn get the right job offers? Have all of us molded by our parents that our education and work ethic matter most been approaching it the wrong way? After all, the Royal Princess snagged William by modeling lingerie at their college fashion show. And she never has to hold down a paying job in her life.

And, so, holding all other variables constant, including education, skills and experience, in 2017, how much of a woman's success depends on our intelligence vs. how physically hot we are?

If a man goes to his boss to fight for the raise, the bonus, the promotion, to provide for his family, he's looked at favorably. If a woman does the same, she's viewed as someone who has failed to secure the right provider.

We already know that pay for the same work isn't equal. The $.85 per dollar statistics haven't changed much since I was in college, and that was the early 90s. We are still single-digit in percentages of CEO table seats held. And, oh yeah, we have that biological clock.

I worked for corporations for twenty years and while of course there have been setbacks and disappointments, I also did get to do and see some pretty fantastic things. My success didn't come easily or accidentally. It was a long, methodical process and all kinds of events had to happen to ensure the corporate climb. Also, I was the lucky one: in those twenty years almost all of my bosses were women.

But what happened when the people in power were men? Some were good. There are a lot of good men – good bosses, good colleagues, good husbands, good fathers, good brothers, good uncles. They hold so much power because they influence the success of the women around them.

And to you, good men, I say thank you.

And there were also the others, the ones who knew they were in power and who knew they liked pretty girls and who would do things, big or small, to take advantage of the situation.

There was the one male teacher I had when I was a teenager. I quickly realized that the only way to get an A in his class was to get his attention. And so I would sit front row, wearing a leather mini skirt. And it worked. I got my desired grade. And then there was the one professor, whose syllabus made it clear that your public answers in the classroom weighed heavily on your grade. The problem was that he either called on men or on the prettiest women in the room. So I did what I had to – I got a tan, wore tight shirts and moved my seat to the front. Again, I got the grade I wanted.

And then there was the manager at a place I worked at while I was still shaping my career. He wasn't my manager, but I had to be in his office a lot. He was married. I was engaged. We both wore rings. This didn't stop him from accidentally knocking things off his desk so that I could bend over and pick them up. And one time reaching towards the back of my neck and saying, "Oh, your sweater tag was hanging out. I fixed it for you."

In each of these cases, I knew the material and did the exact same work as my male peers. But I also played the game. Because as women it's what you do. You push yourself in your field, staying late, working overtime for free, taking it home on weekends, earning extra experience, overlooking the occasional bad behavior, just for the chance to be considered an equal to your male colleagues.

On top of it? You must be hot.

In your 20s and 30s that isn't very difficult. You know, biology. But by the time you hit 40 everything changes. Your body metabolism slows down, your skin sags and your hair turns gray. You start to become invisible. Invisible to the hiring managers. Invisible to the men your age who are divorced and dating women in their 20s. Invisible to the marketers who are happy to pimp Viagra but are terrified of an older women's sexuality.

The recent season (S3) of Grace and Frankie, on Netflix, does a marvelous job of bringing much of this to light. From ergonomic vibrators to bank loan refusals, the comedy, starring Jane Fonda and Lily Tomlin playing 70-something suddenly-single women whose husbands came out of the closet, and leave their wives so that they could be married to each other, holds nothing back from the audience. Because the audience can relate to these truths.

Granted, it's not all gloom and doom. I have several women clients who had tremendous job offers within a few months of us working together. In all cases the women were educated, leaders in their fields, married and with kids. All of them are in great shape, elegant dressers and have gorgeous smiles.

They know how to play the game better than anyone. I have the utmost respect for them.

I had this thought recently. Well, really, for a while now. I'm not proud of it. It's not a thought I feel comfortable sharing publicly. Because everything about this thought goes against everything my inner feminist holds true. After all, growing up I was the tomboy. I played sports. I played the drums. I went to a business school that was 80% male. Most of my students have been men. So I am very comfortable playing in the boys' playground. And, perhaps, this has also backfired on me?

So here's the emotional thought, the ugly realization, the perceived truth: I simultaneously judge and resent the women who get to stay at home while their husbands financially provide for them and their families. They can do all their important volunteer work and be mothers of the year because someone else in their household has to hustle.

Rationally, I do understand that staying at home and taking care of the kids, the house, the budget, the meals, the driving and all of it is totally exhausting. And often unrewarding. And simultaneously both noisy and extraordinarily lonely. It's a 24/7 non-stop obligation ride. I know all kinds of women who have masters degrees, who gave up their professions that they worked really hard to excel in so that they can manage the family in a healthy and positive way. It was a choice made and whether or not they ever return into the workforce will also be a personal and family-needs based decision. How the market will respond to them is a different article.

And this brings me back to the Kate Middleton point. She married into the royal family by modeling lingerie to the future King of England. Do we all learn from her, well, do women in their 20s and 30s, with quick metabolisms, tight skin and good hair? Do we women accept that your best career move is to use your beauty, your body and your sexuality to attract the best kind of breadwinner who will then provide for you for the rest of your life? And then you have the freedom to do whatever you want.

As a single mother of a boy toddler, I'm both grateful and relieved that he will never have to make his life choices driven by his physicality. If he becomes a professional athlete, then yes, of course, but that's the demand of the actual profession. He's already got the tall gene and is a good looking kid. So the world will respond in kind to that. But in the end, whatever profession he does choose, most likely he'll be hired based on his education, his skills and his experience. He'll never have to pose on LinkedIn in a bikini.

I wish it was the same for us women.

This piece was originally published in the HuffPost in April, 2017.

"FORWARD MOTION.
IN BUSINESS. IN RELATIONSHIPS. IN LIFE.
IT'S WHAT DRIVES EVERYTHING."

#LoveWhatYouDo

#CreativeCadence. Strategy. Marketing. Coaching.
Photo/Quote: A. Sukhoy. Cleveland. 2016.

NEXT LEVEL/INSPIRATION

"He who is not courageous enough to take risks will accomplish nothing in life."
— Muhammad Ali

"That's one small step for a man, one giant leap for mankind." – Neil Armstrong

11.1
STEP IT UP

You never know when your next career-altering moment can happen. Perhaps it's at the gym, when the person next to you on the treadmill starts up a discussion and 20 sweaty minutes later you just had an impromptu job interview.

Perhaps it's when a friend invites you to a tech conference and you're suddenly exchanging biz cards with a start-up agency. Or perhaps it's when you receive a call out of the blue because someone who knows you has the confidence that you're the best person for a new assignment.

Regardless of situation, think on your feet, take on the challenge and elevate your career momentum.

Step it up. Quickly.

"There's the psychotic ambitious side of myself that wants a fashion line and my own network and be like a combination of Oprah and Gwen Stefani. And have a perfume. Definitely a perfume."
– Mindy Kaling

11.2
10 IDEAS TO HELP ADVANCE YOUR CAREER.
BACK TO BASICS IN A HIGH-NETWORK WORLD.

Now is a marvelous time to do a career audit and determine if things are on track or if it's time for a change. Regardless of motivation, there's several things we can all do to advance the career path.

1. **Build and Nurture Your LinkedIn Account** – If there's nothing else you plan on doing differently this year, then get this done. And realize it's an on-going process. Recruiters, schools and perspective employers now use LinkedIn as a first stop to scan a potential candidate. Plus, the free version of LinkedIn now also provides a job search menu that currently has a much higher credibility of posts than the clutter often seen on other job sites.

2. **Change Perspective on Facebook** – With over a billion members, Facebook can now connect you to just about everyone you've ever met, since you were a child. And all those connections know people from various industries and firms, in multiple locations, both domestically and internationally. Watch what people are posting and, mostly, watch what you post and make sure the latter is appropriate for your highest level of audience: bosses, students, coworkers, etc. People generally want to help each other out, especially if there's a common bond, and Facebook is the perfect starting place to explore new possibilities.

3. **Reciprocate Generosity** – As I often tell my students, "Don't be that guy, the person who always asks for help / favors / leads / introductions, but never does anything to step up and offer the same." Eventually, people will catch on to which side of the fence you fall and if you're the person on whom others can lean, then they will be much more open to lend a hand to you. It's all about the energy exchange and balance.

4. **It's Not What You Do Online, It's What You Take Offline** – No matter how much social media you use, realize that meeting people in person, over coffee or breaking bread, creates a much stronger relationship foundation than all the emails in the world. Challenge yourself to, at minimum, meet with one new person every single month. What can you learn from him? What can you teach her? How can the two of you help each other succeed?

5. **Invest in Thank You Notes** – Go out and purchase a nice box of Thank You stationery. Look for a professional look, applicable for both male and female recipients, and whenever someone does something kind for you — opens a door, introduces a key contact, reviews your resume — send them a nice, hand-written Thank You note. They won't expect it and chances are, they'll keep it, for awhile, which means they'll keep you on their mind. If budget allows, print monogrammed, blank notes for a personal touch.

6. **Join a Professional Organization** – Whether it's the local chapter of your university, a trade group or a new community initiative, attending on a monthly or quarterly basis will enable you to meet new people with common interests. These people often come from different backgrounds and can provide insight into new trends and directives are unfamiliar to you. And, if you're not finding an organization that peaks your curiosity, start one!

7. **Take a Class. Teach a Class.** – Technology is constantly changing. Companies often require certain skills or certifications. Students ask a lot of questions. By either sitting behind a desk, or by standing in front of a white board, you'll learn something new that you can then apply in your job or that business you always wanted to start. And teaching forces the mind to stretch and ensures you're at the top of a specific subject or trade.

8. **Learn a Language** – The world is getting smaller. American companies are expanding into foreign lands. International firms are opening U.S. branches. They are looking for people that don't just know how to speak the language of choice, but also individuals who understand the local culture, customs and etiquette. And, if speaking anything besides English isn't your cup of tea, then learn how to write computer code, the universal language.

9. **Start a Blog** – True, there's a million blogs out there, with a million bloggers writing whatever they want, some who have a journalism degree and some who just want to express themselves. But who is expressing your voice? Who is communicating your ideas with the world at large? It's one more platform-building avenue and is a perfect social media compliment.

10. **Set Achievable Goals** – While the above ideas are all here to help you advance your career in the new year, they can only help you if you think about and then write down exactly what it is you want to professionally achieve over the next twelve months — promotion, bonus, move. Then determine how the various tools available can help you in achieving these goals.

"I don't have to chase extraordinary moments to find happiness
- it's right in front of me if I'm paying attention and practicing gratitude." – Brene Brown

11.3
GIVING THANKS AND PAYING IT FORWARD:
7 DAYS / 7 WAYS TO HELP ADVANCE SOMEONE ELSE'S CAREER

We don't have to wait till Thanksgiving to reflect on the past year and show our gratitude via kindness towards others. Now is the perfect opportunity to pay it forward and give someone else a leg up on their job search.

Here's a list of ideas that are, for the most part, either free or cost a few minutes of your day.

1. **Connect** – While you may not always be impressed with your own network, for someone starting out or transitioning into a new career space, that one critical contact can mean the difference between being lost and having a plan. If you know two people who are on the opposite experience ends within a specific industry or two professionals with complimentary skill sets, send both a quick note (via email, LinkedIn or Facebook) and let them know the basis of the intro. The rest is up to them.

2. **Sip** – The most important thing you can do with social media isn't what you do online, but what you take offline. Have a cup of coffee with someone who may be struggling or need some advice that you can offer. Not only can you provide encouragement within your line of expertise (or regarding life itself), but you'll also strengthen what could be a long-term relationship. Oh, be sure to listen more and talk less. And realize that it's about them and their present not about you and your past. You're helping someone else build their future.

3. **Write** – With so much negativity on social media, write a favorable review for a local restaurant and another community business. The owners may even feel so proud of your words regarding their service that they may frame it and hang it in their office.

4. **Recommend** – LinkedIn recommendations have shifted from nice-to-haves to must-haves, especially with recruiters and hiring managers. Don't ask someone to write one for you. Instead, surprise someone and write it about them.

5. **Congratulate** – With so many people still struggling with their careers, if you do hear someone receiving the college acceptance letter, diploma, job offer or business loan, send them a personal, hand-written Congratulations note. The fact that you acknowledge their accomplishment and you believe in their future will move self-doubting mountains out of the way and pave the way for future success.

6. **Give** – Perhaps you have some office supplies, fabrics or furniture that once had the best intention of use but no longer hold any value in your home. Collect everything, pack it up and drop it off to someone starting out. You're helping them build their dream, one paperclip at a time.

7. **Love** – That's right, just by loving something or someone, chances are you're already gushing over that person, place or thing. In Corporate America, we call these loyalty lovers Brand Ambassadors, because when you get the word out, especially if you're influential in your community, social or otherwise, your enthusiasm becomes contagious and others crave what brought you that state of euphoria. So keep on loving and others will start to love, too.

Remember, energy is like a boomerang.

Why not let the best come to you by giving the best of yourself to others first?

"You gain strength, courage, and confidence by every experience in which you really stop to look fear in the face. You are able to say to yourself, 'I lived through this horror. I can take the next thing that comes along.'" – *Eleanor Roosevelt*

11.4
LEAD WITH CONFIDENCE

When it comes to your career strategy, my advice to you is to lead with confidence.

It's so easy to hesitate, to question and to hold back. To revert to failed diets, broken promises and unfair job reviews. Instead of being the object of these circumstances, instead let's be the subjects of our lives and pursue the things we want more than anything with new-found *huztpah*.

On your path, you will fall and you will make mistakes. Who cares? Get back up and get going.

- Write down your goals

- Pick the most important one

- Break it down into daily action

- Get the right support system in place

- Track your accomplishments

- Celebrate major milestones

Pretty soon you'll be on your way.

"The old equation of work, rest and play has been replaced by work, work and work." – A. S.

11.5
WHY WORK SABBATICALS MATTER.
10 WAYS TO GET AWAY FROM IT ALL

America is obsessed with work.

Busy is the new Chanel bag. The more busy you are and the more you talk about how busy you are to others, the more important you appear.

Now, more than ever, America should bring back the Sabbatical. And not just for tenure educators. After about six months of careful planning, I gave myself that gift. A self-funded and work-on-the-go sabbatical.

On January 2, 2014, finding a one-day Polar Vortex gap, I got into my car and headed to Chicago. Once there I spent one month with my family, helping my Sis plan her wedding and catching up with friends.

On February 4, I hopped on a plane and via a connecting flight arrived in Dublin, Ireland, where I spent the next three and a half weeks exploring Emerald City. Upon return, and after a brief one-week stay in the Midwest, I hopped on another plane and arrived in Florida, where I stayed with my cousin in his Coral Springs home for the next three weeks. After that I flew to Austin, Texas, which was supposed to be home next. Instead, it was a four-week adventure. Finally, from Austin I flew to Cancun, Mexico, where together with family I celebrated my sister's and brother-in-law's wedding.

By the time I took the three flights back, revisiting most of my hubs (Cancun/Austin/Chicago/Cleveland) to the 216, it had been one third of 2014 on planes, trains and automobiles. An amazing once in a lifetime journey across the globe.

Some people close to me didn't understand my decisions or my lifestyle. They still don't. And that's okay. When you're Old School from the Old Country, you go to the job. The job doesn't go to you. But today we live in a modern economy, a disruptive economy that enables tremendous flexibility, provided you're a good planner.

I didn't really understand the why of it all myself when everything began. All I knew, at the time, was I wanted to move to Austin: no city taxes, no state taxes, warm weather, live music capitol of the world, thriving business. I also realized if I wasn't going to pay rent down there for a while, I might as well pay rent overseas.

Thus the opportunity for Dublin. But it was only after all those airplane takeoffs and landings I realized that the soul knew something the mind hadn't yet realized: I was burnt out.

I love teaching. I love career coaching. And, within four and a half years, I taught nearly 900 students and coached over 100 clients — that's 1000 people whose careers I worked very hard to advance. Who was working to advance mine? As adjunct faculty, I didn't have the option to get a paid sabbatical, something reserved for the shrinking number of tenures, who have to apply for it and then have committees approve it.

I reached a certain point in 2013 when I realized I didn't have much to give to others anymore. And that I had to work so much harder just to generate the same results. Because my mind was out of steam. The brain disk wasn't so much full as it was empty.

I'm grateful I listened to the intuitive side of myself to make the journey to two continents, three countries and six cities a reality. And, I also realize it's not something someone can just get up and do.

Here's what I had to do to make it happen:

1. **Coordinate Your Contracts** – I knew my apartment lease, my car lease and my school contract were all ending ~end of December. This was the perfect exit trifecta.

2. **Sell Everything. Almost Everything** – By the time 2013 was wrapping up, I had donated or sold every piece of furniture I owned. The two exceptions? The custom globe my sis once ordered me and the ergonomic computer chair I got on a double-deep discount at Staples. The rest of my stuff found its way into boxes and storage. And a generous friend who let me keep most of it at her house.

3. **Save Your Money** – I planned financially and made sure I had enough in the bank to take me where I needed to be for a certain amount of time.

4. **Track the Prices** – I shopped for flight pricing every single day for one month. Until one day I found the ticket sweet spot: $590 for the round trip to Dublin. I also passed up on the high-ticket hotel rentals and, instead, sublet a room via Airbnb. The penthouse suite location was cheaper than the very cheapest hotel in Dublin, not to mention owned by a great hostess that became a friend. And, one exception, in cities I visited I either paid cheap rent to people I knew or paid no rent at all.

5. **Work Remotely** – Since I don't have a rich uncle or trust fund, I was able to continue to work with my clients from every single place I stayed at, including Dublin. And thanks to PayPal, and my Sis, who would deposit client checks, I continued to earn money - working, interviewing, writing - no matter where I was. Coffee shops make the best remote offices.

6. **Pack Lightly** – I could live on whatever would fit in one suitcase, a vanity bag and computer bag. As long as I had access to laundry, I was good to go.

7. **Skip the Souvenirs** – I didn't need to buy stuff where I was. Not saying I lived on $20 a day, because I didn't. Food, everywhere, is expensive. But, instead of the need to buy things to show-off to others where I had been, I turned to my creative tools and blogged, took photos, shot videos and even kept a journal to document my observations. To me, this form of memory-making is far more fun than stuffing a suitcase full of pricey tourist *tchatchkis*.

8. **Load Up On Apps** – I took advantage of all the technology out there, filling my iPhone with apps that I relied on heavily, but only using them where free WiFi was available. So whether PayPal, Viber, Waze, United, SouthWest or my bank, at any given moment, I knew where I stood, geographically and financially. And when need be, made split second decisions.

9. **Invest in Quality Shoes** – Every city I lived in I walked. As in everywhere. In Chicago I took the El and walked from the stops to wherever I had to go. In Dublin I walked 3 – 5 hours a day. In Coral Springs I walked to the gym, the Starbucks and the grocery store. In Austin, I walked where I could, then would hop on a bus to take me elsewhere. No car rental for me, thank you.

10. **Know When to Say When** – The travel had a finite point. Granted, my original plan was to stay in Austin, but as I returned to Cleveland in mid-May, I also knew that inside, the travel clock reached its course and it was time to get off on a platform to stay grounded, at least until the itch to pull the passport scratches once more.

The journey – and my professional and life productivity - had been nothing short of incredible: I met great people from all over the globe, spent more time with my family than I had since 2001, finished two books that were four years in the making, talked shop with (the now late) John Hurt, built muscle in my legs and witnessed my parents walk my sister down the aisle.

I am fully aware that all of this was tremendous gift. Mostly, what this Sabbatical — which was anything but restful — did for me is a gift that, back on January 2, 2014, I never saw coming: it re-energized the soul battery. And by dropping out of everything, it brought me back to me.

"PLAN BEYOND YOUR CURRENT OBSTACLES."

#CREATIVECADENCE
#DateYourCareer
photo: a. sukhoy

OVERCOMING OBSTACLES

"It's our challenges and obstacles that give us layers of depth and make us interesting. Are they fun when they happen? No. But they are what make us unique. And that's what I know for sure...I think." – Ellen DeGeneres

"We were never supposed to live until 40. We were built to self-destruct at 30, whether from cancer or mental illness. We're all going way beyond our expiration date." – Douglas Coupland

12.1
I'M MENTALLY ILL. PLEASE HIRE ME.
BY DEENA NYER MENDLOWITZ

Dear Employer,

Hi. I'm Deena and I'm mentally ill. Please hire me.

I want to be clear, I'm not asking you to take pity on me and hire me because I'm mentally ill. I have plenty of people who will take pity on me, I don't need any more. No, I am saying I am mentally ill. I am open about it and don't feel the need to hide behind shame (a ridiculous idea, I know,) and you should hire me because I will be one of the best employees you've ever had.

But you're mentally ill, you're thinking, that sounds scary, you could go crazy at work, or always call in sick or be less productive because of your illness, or you could be sad all the time and be a total drag.

I hear you and I'll answer these concerns one at a time.

What if you go crazy and scream or just lose it?

I'm not the employee you need to worry about, in fact I'm the exact opposite because I actually get the help I need. I'm someone who has identified my illness, sought treatment, and is aware of how I am doing. The people who fly off the handle and make your life difficult, they are the ones not seeking treatment, and they're probably not because they're afraid of the stigma, especially workplace stigma.

I bet you call in sick a lot or are less productive cause you're depressed.

Have I missed work because of depression? Yes, but very rarely, and not to lay on the couch or because "I just wasn't up to it." The person who called in "sick" to binge watch all seven seasons of Gilmore Girls so they were caught up for the Netflix reunion show has already been hired by your company, and that's not me. I am like someone who has diabetes or Crohn's, I come in every single

148

day unless I require medical attention and even if that happens I've still worked from a hospital or home.

The unnecessary guilt I have about living with this disease and also the feeling of not wanting to let people down, those feelings will actually work to your advantage because I want to be your best employee to get rid of any doubts or misconceptions you may have about mental illness.

Yeah, but if you're depressed you're probably a total buzzkill and sad all the time.

Your office already has a sad person, every office does. But that's not me. I'm a delight. Really. Depression gets a bad rap. People think you're an Eeyore always walking around bemoaning life, but that person is a pessimist, not someone with mental illness. Me? I'm a Tigger, a Tigger who might think about death a little more than I should (hey, I'm going for honesty here) but who leaves those thoughts for the professionals I see and the friends I message post-work. At the office I'm the hard worker, doing what you ask and more, making jokes when appropriate, and texting you on the way in to ask if you want a Starbucks.

So as I said, I'm Deena and I'm mentally ill. Please hire me.

References (from past employers and therapists) available upon request.

I wrote the cover letter above in August of 2016 after being under-employed for over a year. During that time I had been looking for jobs primarily in social media. I had proven experience. In fact the social media content refresh I did for my last job was featured in *AdAge Magazine*. But even after that feature, our company decided to outsource social media and nearly our whole department was let go in one day.

So, I was back on the career-dating scene.

I was bummed to be leaving this work relationship as I found it satisfying, comforting, and felt my contributions mattered and were recognized, which is what we all want in a relationship, right? But sometimes you're at the right place at the wrong time so you part ways.

One of the places I met with while job searching was a placement company that specializes in filling creative positions for companies. In addition to my recent work, I had also freelanced for advertising agencies, and been a best-selling humor greeting card writer so my portfolio was full. I showed the woman at the placement agency my work and she was impressed by it and then as I was about to leave she said, "My one concern is if someone Googles your name, the first thing they would see is your website. You might want to think if you're okay with that."

The woman was kind and shared this concern tactfully and it was something I had thought about before. Yet it was still disheartening to have it confirmed. My website is called *Funnel Cakes Not Included*. It is a blog and also contains information about my play. Both said blog and play are primarily about living with mental illness, finding the humor in it, and attempting to get rid of the shame and stigma associated with it.

I am immensely proud of this website and of my decision to be open about living with mental illness. I am also aware it has cost me jobs.

After this woman shared her concerns I was left with two options:
1. Take my website down till I found a new job or
2. Leave it up knowing the ramifications

I decided to leave it up for two reasons:
1. I knew it has helped people living with mental illness find a place of empathy and it helped their family and friends learn how to be more supportive of them
2. Because of how it helped my previous employers understand and advocate for me while I was ill and working for and with them

As I was writing *AdAge* worthy tweets that combined selling vacuums with references to *Napoleon Dynamite*, *Saved by the Bell*, and *Orange is the New Black*, that same brain that was silly and creative was also struggling with suicidal thoughts. In my tenure at this company I would require multiple hospital stays, shock therapy, and an outpatient treatment program. I would write tweets and social media posts for my employer from all these places.

When I was in the office one day I received an e-mail from my department head. My boss had found my website and shared it with her and she wrote me a note that among other things said *"I have read your intelligent, brave, and generous blog. It helped me understand and therefore accept. Keep fighting — your many gifts may have come at a high price but the world is a better place because people like you are in it."*

When I would get discouraged with my job search and question my decision to be so open about my mental illness, I would always come back to her message. The fact that I was able to help one person, a person who is in charge of hiring and managing employees, see mental illness differently and the people who live with it as smart, competent, valued assets to a company, was all the motivation I needed to keep my website up and to continue my job search.

I recently found a full-time job teaching pre-school. While it isn't great for the bank account, it is wonderful for the mind, body, and soul. The position is a natural fit even though my degree is not in education. I have been teaching kids improv for years, I have spent the last ten years raising my wonderful son and also I have spent the last four years teaching people every day how to better understand mental illness.

Living with this disease, I've been reminded that what makes us most healthy as adults starts with who we get to be as children, and now every day I get to be a part of that process. And though my relationship with this school is still in the early phase, I'm seeing a long-term partner all the way.

"There are certainly a lot of things that still need to change when it comes to women in the workforce."
– Dolly Parton

12.2
REFLECTIONS ON THE HARDSHIP OF BEING
AN ACTIVE MEMBER OF TODAY'S WORKFORCE
BY CORPORATE EXECUTIVE
(WHO WISHES TO REMAIN ANONYMOUS)

I once heard an interview with a famous actor where he discussed a failed movie shortly after winning an Oscar just a year before. Instead of being apologetic, he simply stated that sometimes you need to make a movie, regardless of quality, because you need money. I love the simple truth of that explanation because many of us can relate it to the ups and downs of careers in the corporate world.

Let's face it, most of us are either not fortunate enough or not equipped to land in an ideal situation. And even if we do, corporate environments can change like the weather – just ask anyone who has survived reorganizations, acquisitions and change in management

So just like that actor, choosing to make that awful movie, we too make compromises, because it's the right choice under the circumstances. In career planning there's the ideal of finding the right match, environment and culture. Yet there's little mention of how searching for that ideal situation needs to be balanced against availability of jobs in your area, economic downturns and personal circumstances.

If you have a mortgage, college tuition bills, daycare expenses or aging parents to care for, pragmatism has to rule. So you make a deliberate choice for money, even if that choice puts you in the wrong circumstances. And that should never be held against you if you can contribute and show results.

I carry a vision and hope of finding a perfect setting where my ambition and hard work are perfectly synchronized with that intangible quality, that chemistry that makes me jump out of bed every morning, eager to go to work. I've worked in these environments and they can give you the ready rush of winning an Oscar.

What happens when your job search results in opportunities that are less than ideal? You settle and take that risk. You also choose to meet your responsibilities and you set your intention to succeed. Sometimes you land in the middle of cultural or organization changes that are bigger than your role and completely not under your control. Suddenly, you have one or two of these experiences and you dread being labeled a "job hopper." There are too many stories of companies that hire, and even relocate people only to restructure or eliminate their jobs soon after bringing new people on board.

I don't think organizations do this deliberately, our world moves too fast now and organizations have to respond and adjust accordingly. I do think hiring managers can be naive when they disqualify applicants solely for frequent job changes. Some of us are deliberate risk takers who have to make choices within certain constraints to meet our responsibilities. Surely that is worth some consideration especially during economically and politically turbulent times?

"(My childhood ambition was) to get out of where I was." – Martin Scorsese

12.3
I AM YOU.
BY ERIC DUNN, M.B.A., OSM

I am you.

Whether you are a dreamer; a kid surrounded by poverty, who is told that those dreams are not reality; the student who must work full-time, while also going to school full-time to support yourself; the mid-career professional who has had to go back to school in order to further your career; or maybe the person who is looking to find their way out of a dead-end situation—I am you. I know your struggle and I am here to tell you there is light at the end of the tunnel.

I grew up in the Mount Pleasant neighborhood of Cleveland. It is one of the poorest, lowest educated, highest crime rate areas in the city. It has also been my home for much of my life. Although my father was in my life, my mom raised me as a single mother, and I bore first hand witness to the struggles that it included. She had quite the task to steer me along the right path while being surrounded by family and friends who chose the streets as their route to quick cash and a fast lifestyle. Coming of age during the crack epidemic of the late '80s and early '90s, I bore first hand witness to the effects it can have on a household. I saw people close to me who lived on both sides of the coin, as dealers and users. However, even in my young age, I knew that was not the life I wanted for myself.

Fast forward to 2001. I graduated high school (barely, with a 1.7 GPA) and had no idea what direction I wanted to go in life. Sure, I had a few stints working for a few companies, but I quickly realized that without a solid education, for me, my options would be limited. I was at an impasse. I didn't necessarily love school, but also didn't want to spend the rest of my life struggling to make ends meet.

Then came the moment that would change my life forever. I had someone close to me tell me that I was wasting my life. That I was worthless. Were they right? Did I have no value? For a brief moment, giving into the negativity, I contemplated giving up. But then I heard a voice that said, "If you are already at the bottom, what do you have to lose if you aim for the mountain top? If you end up back here, at least you know you tried."

It was as if a light-bulb went off. I realized that giving up was not an option and the next day I enrolled into college.

From the moment I entered Cuyahoga Community College in pursuit of an Associate's degree in English, to the day I walked across the stage to accept my Masters in Business Administration, this kid who barely graduated high school with a 1.7 GPA, has never ended a semester with anything lower than a 3.5 GPA.

How was I able to accomplish this feat? I will be the first to tell you there is nothing inheritably remarkable about me. I am just a normal guy. However, I am a normal guy that won't accept "I can't" as an answer. I will myself to find a way. Have I had failures? Yes, plenty of them. In fact, one of the most important keys to success is to never fear failure. Embrace it. In every failure exists the ability to learn how to convert that "No" into a "Yes." I have enjoyed success in pivoting my career from one industry to another and building my experience, while also establishing a pathway to entrepreneurship. While by no means have I reached my ultimate goal, I am well on my way.

Early Years

As a youth, I always had ambition. In high school, I would make customized CDs for people charging about $1 per song, with a 12-song minimum. I used this money to help finance my other interest at the time: videogames. During that same period, I also launched my own videogame website that focused solely on upcoming wrestling games. I spent an entire summer teaching myself HTML on the fly to build and design my page. The first iteration of it would be disastrous.

My initial "industry" contact turned out to be fraudulent. This hurt my reputation within the online gaming community. Not to be deterred and learning from my mistakes, I relaunched and re-branded my gaming news site, as an e-mail based newsletter. I grew my subscriber base by being active on message boards of larger sites. Eventually, my subscriber list would exceed nearly 200 members. Not bad for a 14-year-old kid. This level of exposure garnered the attention of one of the biggest wrestling game sites at the time. They extended an offer to join their editorial team and ultimately absorbed my content for their site. In exchange for my services, they would send me free game demos and grant me access to game developers and producers. I thought I was on top of the world, but soon reality would set in.

Within a year into my stint with the new site, things started to unravel between the co-founders of the site. The page had grown to become quite valuable. Keep in mind, this is 1997 amid the dot-com bubble, and this website was garnering nearly one million unique visitors monthly. As the money came in, greed showed its face as the staff started to realize how much we were being cut-out of the windfall the founders enjoyed. This ultimately led to the dissolution of the site. While it was a bitter pill to learn that I was being taken advantage of, it was here that garnered my desire to learn more about business, to ensure that I would never be taken advantage of again.

Professional Career

I have since held multiple positions at varying levels across several industries. I started out as a package handler for a Fortune 500 logistics company, and as of this writing, my current position is an Information Systems business analyst with a software company. A huge jump, right? How was I able to do this? Did I have someone who worked on the inside put me into a position? Did I suck up to the boss to make my way to the top? Was it just dumb luck? The answer to all of these questions is no. The way I was able to accomplish this jump can be easily replicated from individual to individual, and situation to situation.

I was able to accomplish gradual upward mobility in my career because I gained experience from dating my career.

During the dating process, we find ourselves meeting someone, figuring out their likes/dislikes, and going on multiple dates, until you find someone you think is the right fit. Well, this is the same process that occurs within our careers. When I first started out in college, I thought I was going to be a writer, then a psychologist. However here I am today as an analyst. Did I give up? No, I hold degrees that are related to each profession. However, as I went through the process of acquiring those degrees, I realized that maybe there was something out there that was a better fit for me.

Along the way, each career focus provided experience that would shape my next career move. Much as what one wants out of a relationship changes over time, so did my desires of what I wanted out of my career. What I found was that, as I "dated" each discipline, I found things that I loved about them. Conversely, I also uncovered things that didn't appeal to me as much. Being someone who is not afraid of change, I sought out opportunities that aligned closer to what I was seeking. With each new opportunity, however, I brought the lessons I learned along the way, so as not to repeat past mistakes. It is through this iterative learning process that I am able to continuously cultivate my career and get closer to the career I envision for myself.

The Power of the Pivot

The ability and willingness to pivot at critical times, has been one of the most beneficial attributes during my career. It is part skill, part awareness, and part dumb luck. The skill aspect is the ability to expand your skillset. The more diverse one's skills are, the more opportunities you create for yourself. Awareness, is a tacit ability to "read the tealeaves" so to speak. It's the ability to understand changes in your micro and macro environments, and strategically position yourself to adjust as the changes come.

Dumb luck happens, when you recognize an opportunity that lands in your lap without seeking it. Many of us encounter at least one circumstance where we are given an opportunity at an in-opportune time. It is the ability to say yes, when saying no would be more favorable, that will take you furthest in life. It also gives you the opportunity to discover things about yourself you wouldn't have otherwise known.

Making the jump from package handler to IS business analyst was fueled by the drive to build know-how. Instead of working to gather titles, I focused on gaining experience. Moreover, that experience should include building knowledge, skills, and abilities (KSAs) that fall outside the scope of your direct responsibilities. For example, as a package handler at Fed Ex, I would frequently talk to the maintenance team whenever something went wrong. I engaged them about the problem and how they were going to solve it. Now I was a package handler. The questions and their subsequent answers were of no real concern for my position at the time, and were well out of scope for my paygrade. However, knowing I aspired for more, gaining insights into topics above my paygrade was exactly what I wanted. I could have simply gone and chatted it up with other package handlers as many of my peers did; however, I instead chose to use the time to learn more about the bigger picture.

This line of thinking eventually landed me the role as the team lead. It was my willingness to go the extra mile for insight and building my level of practice and action that propelled me forward in my career. To this day, I still engage individuals whose job may or may not be related to what I do, because there is value in understanding the big picture.

Ultimately, what I want you to take away from my story is that anything is possible as long as you believe. One of my favorite sayings is "Whether you believe you can or you cannot, either way, you are right." I come from very humble beginnings and have faced some pretty unrelenting challenges. However, one thing I realize is that the world doesn't stop spinning for anyone. As Alex's MBA professor once taught her, and then she taught us, "Markets never rest." No matter what obstacle you are facing, you either rise to the occasion or it will pass you. Its harsh, its brash, but its life.

When times are hard and it seems like you can't go any further-- have faith. Whether it's in a higher power or it's just in yourself, believe that you can bring your vision to reality. Look around you. Nearly everything that surrounds you was once a vision in someone's mind that they believed they could make reality. Everything from the floorplan of the structure you are currently in, to the words on this page, it all started with a vision. Now it's your turn, to make your vision reality.

Here are a few keys to success, many of which are echoed throughout this book:

- **Have Humility** – Humble yourself. Show the same level of respect you command, whether pauper or president.

- **Do Not Idolize** – While you always want to hold the utmost respect to others, never place anyone above you, or you will always subjugate yourself, and how can you surpass that which you worship?

- **Write Down Your Ideas** – By writing down the things you wish to accomplish, you are transferring them from ideas in your mind, to something tangible in the real world.

- **Learn From the Mistakes of Others** – Never exalt yourself above another's mistake. The biggest fallacy one can make is the notion that "it can't happen to me." While you should never limit yourself based on the success of others, do take note of what works and what doesn't work and adjust your strategy as needed.

- **Never Fear Failure** – No one has never taken a loss in life. It is natural.

- **Don't Be Afraid to Jump** – While you must always move cautiously, never let fear condemn you standing still. In nature, anything that sits for too long eventually becomes stale and stagnant. If opportunity presents itself don't let fear prevent you from making that leap.

- **Surround Yourself With Positive People** – It is imperative that you build relationships with positive people in your life. There will be valleys and peaks on your journey, and having people that can guide you through the storms and keep you level during your high-points, will help keep you heading in the right direction.

- **Build With Those Who Believe in Your Vision** – No success story is built without the inclusion of others. Every "self-made" person has had someone give them a positive reinforcement around their ideas; whether it be someone who extended them a job offer, mentored them, or a customer who gave their product a try. Seek out others who also have vision and work together to make those visions reality.

Conquering the unknown takes guts. It's why so few set sail.

#MarchForward

Photo: a. sukhoy. Dublin. 2014.

#CREATIVECADENCE
STRATEGY. MARKETING. COACHING.

INDUSTRY DISRUPTORS

"Whether it's steamships disrupted by the railroads or railroads disrupted by the airlines, it's typically the large entrenched incumbents that are displaced by innovators." – Peter Diamandis

"You know I don't repeat myself." - *Madonna*

13.1
10 CAREER LESSONS FROM MADONNA

In September, 2015 I had the incredible experience of seeing Madonna in concert at Chicago's United Center. My lifelong friend Chris Forillo bought floor-seat tickets, nestled perfectly between the stage and the runway. While a lifelong fan of the Material Girl, the last time I had the pleasure to see her live was back in late August, 2001, also with Chris as well as my Sis and cousin Jen.

Madonna was touring to promote her Rebel Heart album and while she performed a lot of the new numbers, with the exception of "Music," she mostly flipped between the new songs and, to her fans' delight, the vintage ones, like "Burning Up," "Like a Virgin," "Dress You Up" and encoring with the classic "Holiday."

She had more costume changes than I could count, and shifted themes and genres quickly, from intimate ballads, to Flamenco versions of her classic numbers to closing out the show in a Great Gatsby inspired Art Deco party.

At one point in the final act of the show, Madonna, dressed in a stunning beaded flapper dress, acknowledged that the tour features a lot of dancers, musicians and theatrics. She was sitting on the end of the red velvet stage with a guitar in hand and, surprising thousands of her guests, began an intimate, pared-down performance of "La Vie En Rose," sung entirely in French. I have goose bumps writing about it.

That's the beauty of Madonna - she does what she wants and how she wants it. Her 30+ year career, as both a creative force and a business brain, has inspired a new generation of artists, infused discourse in numerous college marketing courses and fueled the inspiration for some of us with an independent streak to follow suit, in whatever industry we chose.

I've adored her from the very beginning, vividly recalling her first appearance on Dick Clark's American Bandstand in 1984. The music industry veteran asked the then novice what her goals are. The girl in the black tights, thrift-shop skirt and cut-off shirt smiled mischievously into the microphone and prophetically replied, "To rule the world."

Her ambitions, talent and perseverance assured her goal was met.

So what can all of us learn from her? A list of 10 Career Lessons from Madonna:

1. **Have a Vision** - Markets never rest and neither does Madonna. She consistently brings her visions to life and pushes the boundaries of what's expected. The result? Triggering people's senses, morals and internal codes of what's permissible and possible.

2. **Work Hard** - When Henry Rollins was interviewed on VH1 regarding Madonna, he said that when the rest of us are sleeping, resting or eating, Madonna is working. He was right. She doesn't have to work anymore. She wants to.

3. **Shut Off the Noise** - Madonna has had more haters than any other modern musical artist. Critics have trashed everything about her. 35 years later? She's laughing all those critics to the bank. And to the sold-out concert arenas. Because her fans? Well, we love her.

4. **Risk the Sandbox** - Madonna's true talent isn't her singing voice, she'll be the first to admit so. Rather, it's that she sings, dances, writes her own songs, plays instruments, acts, directs, writes kids books, designs clothes and will execute her drive on any medium that she chooses. She doesn't obsess about failures. She knows they're just a numbers game to success.

5. **Balance the Yin and the Yang** - Across her career, specifically her musical contributions, her songs have spanned the spectrum, from the fun to the profound. For every dance track that's attached to her name, she also gave us "Oh, Father," "Express Yourself" and the recent (and reflective) "HeartBreak City." She knows there's time to celebrate and time to contemplate.

6. **Align Yourself with Leaders** - When she first arrived in NYC, Madonna started spending time with the city's emerging creative class: Jean-Michel Basquiat, Jellybean Martinez and Keith Haring, among others. This opened all kinds of doors and helped propel her forward. Today Madonna collaborates with a variety of artists because she understands that cross-over appeal matters.

7. **Love What You Do** - Whether Madonna's in the studio or on stage or in an interview, what's evident is her passion. She's genuinely in the moment and as she storms the stage in stilettos, strutting along dancers half her age, she's the one in charge.

8. **Look Good** - Madonna was one of the pioneers of image in the MTV era. She knew looks mattered, especially for women and, instead of cursing the double standard between the sexes, she flipped it on its head, cultivating each physical reincarnation into a media talking point.

9. **Have a Sense of Humor** - Madonna may not be the world's best comedian, but she's funny when she wants to be and, more importantly she knows when to filter the serious from the *drek*. The result? When the latter lands on her doorstep, she just laughs it off. And moves on. Because lingering takes away from work.

10. **Live Your Life Your Way** - Madonna was born into a conservative, Catholic, Midwest family. She even briefly attended the University of Michigan on a dancing scholarship before giving up all sense of existing security and projected expectations to move to NYC to pursue her dreams. And ever since, she defined the rules of her life.

Today's leading women in the male-dominated music industry – Taylor Swift, Beyonce, Lady Gaga, Miley Cyrus – have much to thank her for – she paved the way for them. Just as Debbie Harry, Grace Jones and Chrissie Hynde did before her.

Not all of us have Madonna's *hutzpah*. Each of us has our own vision, career and life to pursue. How do we know we're in the right zone? When others start looking to us to define their professional journey.

As Henry Rollins shared in a 2011 interview in MadonnaRama, "She didn't flinch. She stood down the world. She did it her way and continues to. She always wins and because of her, countless millions have been inspired."

The Material Girl would agree. But she's too busy working.

"The first time I stepped on an NBA court I became a businessman." – LeBron James

13.2
THE BIG CAREER LESSON OF LEBRON JAMES

Summer 2016. The city of Cleveland celebrates its first major sports team victory in over 50 years. Thanks to the Cavs unprecedented 1-3 turnaround, led by LeBron James, the city of the underdog, full of generational sports – and industry and population – disappointments, now lifts its head and carries it high, in pride. So this is what winning feels like?

I first moved to Cleveland back in 2003, LeBron's draft year. Wanting to right the wrong of never having attended a Michael Jordan Bulls game while growing up in Chicago, I made sure I got myself to the Gund Arena (now the Q) as much as possible. Plus, I lived in downtown Cleveland, at the Statler, a full decade before it became the hip thing to do.

In Fall of 2003, LeBron's first season, my childhood friend Erin came to visit. We were both on the jr. high basketball team back in the 80s and loved the sport. We walked to the stadium and enjoyed our seats. That was the first game they scored over 100 points. We knew we were watching something special. We also yelled at the refs' calls.

In the decade since his arrival, the Cavs, the city and life went thru more ups and downs than the most twisty of roller coasters. In 2010, post economic crash and LeBron's dumping of Cleveland for the more sexy Miami, the overall psychology of the 216 simultaneously felt more desperate and more confident. It shifted gears to another focus. It had to. We all did.

With Michael Symon winning the Iron Chef in 2007, Cleveland and all us foodies focused on the culinary scene. And here's where Cleveland was ahead of the game. As brick and mortar retail continues to spiral, a full decade prior to, this town began to fill its empty store front with eateries that brought in European and Asian cuisine, as well as the trendiness of East and West coasts. N.E. Ohio born chefs traveled to different corners of the earth and returned home, bringing what they learned and then serving it up to their people with the Cleveland lens: big portions, unpretentious service and in taverns and bistros that fostered social interaction and ensured good times.

Over those beef cheek pierogis at Lola's on East 4th Street, we, the passionate people of C-Town, discussed politics, the economy and, of course, sports.

What LeBron did to secure our win last night was no different from what the chefs of these establishments did. Some of us were just too naïve and heart-broken seven years ago to fully understand the strategy. The man had a plan from the get go.

In order to have a winning team, he first had to know what it meant to win. And in order to do that, he abandoned home and, like Dorothy, went to a new land and made new friends and learned to play and defeat on new territory. He won two back-to-back championships in 2012 and 2013 and only then, he was ready to show his home team how that happens.

He returned in 2014 and promised us the big win. I had just returned from my own global travels including a one-month writing sabbatical in Dublin, Ireland. Just one year later the Cavs advanced to the finals. Right about then I discovered I was going to have a baby. And just one year after that they won the big trophy. It was a spectacular Game 7 that I enjoyed watching with my six-month old son.

In the seconds after the final buzzer of that 2016 game, an emotional LeBron got down on his knees and wept. Anyone who has ever criticized him – and there have been many, including this writer – had to swallow some pride because they knew he and his team earned this victory. And winning it away – on another team's home turf – made the win even sweeter. We are now the NBA standard.

The big career lesson we can all learn from LeBron is if we want to be the very best at what we do, sometimes we must risk everything, leave it all behind and go explore what winners do and how they do it.

Whether in sports or in cooking or in music or anything else that gives our souls the purpose to get up in the morning and to support ourselves and our families, learning how the rest of the world delivers on and excels in our craft and then making all that our own, that's how we win at our profession.

That's how we win at life.

This piece was originally published in the HuffPost in the Summer of 2017.

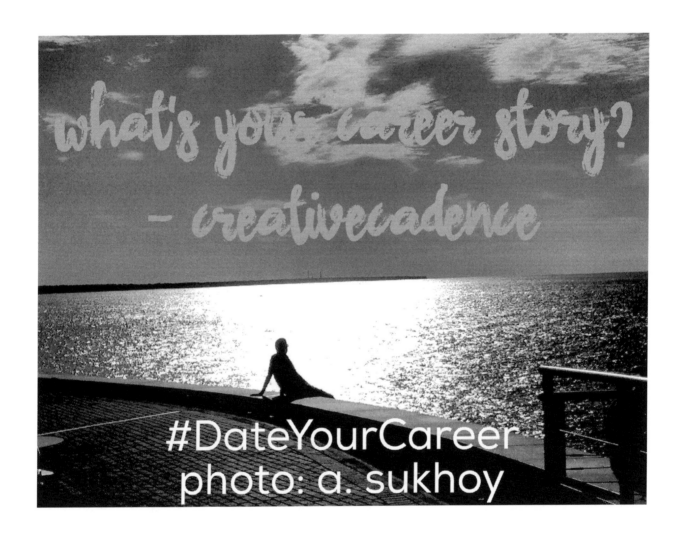

what's your career story?
– creativecadence

#DateYourCareer
photo: a. sukhoy

FINAL WORDS

*"The top experts in the world are ardent students.
The day you stop learning, you're definitely not an expert." — Brendon Burchard*

"A man's worth is no greater than his ambitions." – *Marcus Aurelius*

14.1
FINAL WORDS
BY PAUL IBRAHIM, M.B.A.

Alex is the rare person who embodies exactly what she preaches, and her successes strongly reflect this genuine character. When we first met in the Fall of 2013, it was just the beginning of my MBA studies at Cleveland State University. Looking back, this could not have been more opportune time to meet. Alex took the dream of starting a business and showed the path to make it a reality.

I had always known that I loved "business" as if "business" was this thing you could ask Santa for. When I was three years old and my father asked me what I want to be when I grew up, without hesitation, I responded with, "CEO."

But what did that mean? It wasn't until Alex blew the doors off my limiting mindset that I started to understand.

Alex had us study the classic business cases – the Rockefellers, the Dukes, the Astors and then the Brins, Zuckerbergs, Pages and Sandbergs of the world. But we also studied some not-so-standard models, like Vladimir Putin and Lady Gaga. In fact, our first team-selected leadership project subject was Mr. Putin, who, in Fall of 2013, on the eve of the Crimean Crisis, was a far timelier choice than my then teammate and now good friend Chris Connelly and I could have imagined.

One of Putin's pivotal life moments was meeting a professor named Anatoly Sobchak, while studying economic law in his mid-twenties. After his KGB tour in Germany, Putin returned to St. Petersburg and was quickly given an advisor's role to the now-mayor Sobchak. But Putin had to be open and then willing to listen and take advantage of this chance networking encounter.

After all the teams presented on their self-chosen leaders, Alex deconstructed these titans down to their basic elements. Exactly why we studied these figures was a true game changer. What is it that made these people successful? How could Angela Merkel, Sheryl Sandberg, Jennifer Lopez and James Buchanan Duke have common traits?

Each of these names stands on its own as a brand. Alex is the first person who spoke to us of the personal brand and its importance. Your online fingerprints - your network, your resume, your cover letters, and your persona - are all part of your personal brand, and if your brand is weak, you will not succeed. First Vanderbilt, Carnegie and Roosevelt, then Disney and today Putin and Gaga all viciously defend their brands and intentionally cultivate a specific image. This book contains the blueprint for a huge portion of that critical work.

It went far beyond their extravagances and wealth – those are the results of their similarities, not the cause. All these self-starters had critical mentors in their lives and experienced critical events that, via irreversible and risky choices, propelled them on their paths. And all of them acted decisively when presented with opportunity. None of them modified their behavior based on some popularity contest. They knew exactly who they are, what they wanted and how to get there, obstacles be damned.

They were, and some still are, without question, the hardest workers of their industries and times.

Let me say this clearly – if you think Warren Buffet and Oprah don't have a ton in common, take a second look

Alex opened a door that will never shut again.

At the end of our class, Alex dropped a bomb on us, or so it seemed at the time. She was leaving. Initial distress quickly gave way to an abundance of inspiration as the details of her plan emerged, including a writing sabbatical to Ireland, among other things. This is the stuff dreams are made of. This was a person who practiced what they preached; a corporate executive leader, who had seen the darker side of business during downsizing, and mastered every step in between. This was someone whose advice I could truly follow, someone who showed exactly what it means to "lead strongly" and to find a way to personally grow out of seemingly "bad" events. This growth and adaptation to obstacles is a hallmark of success.

Fast forward three years and my career and I are going steady, and dare I say, are in love.

My partners and I have our own company that we're currently launching, I have worked with several industry leaders, learning from some great business minds in my career, and I've landed a dream gig at the automotive icon my dad worked at for 37 years. There truly is a formula to follow regardless of your aspirations – whether to climb the ladder or to start a new industry. That formula is outlined clearly in this text.

Reading this book can be one of your major critical events, if you act on it.

No one will hand you your dream job or dream life. You must go out and take it.

Don't be a casualty of rigid thinking and refusal to adapt. As Benjamin Franklin said "To succeed, jump as quickly at opportunities as you do at conclusions."

Jump at yours. You have nothing to lose and literally everything to gain. If one opportunity doesn't materialize as you expected, so what? Get up, brush off and move onto the next one. While you're feeling bad for yourself, someone else is meeting the career love of your life and sweeping it off its feet.

Remember that there are endless opportunities, but you must work to create them for yourself, as you've begun to do with this text.

Your next steps?

- **Network** – Every single moment is an opportunity to network and build relationships.

- **Mentor(s)** – The more the merrier; learn from those who have what you want.

- **Work Hard** – Still the ultimate currency for respect and results.

- **Read** – Start with 10 minutes per day, perhaps before bed. You will be shocked at the impact

- **Listen** – Your inner 4 year-old, they're usually right, and unfettered by the nagging distractions that fill our daily lives.

By doing the above you'll demonstrate the most attractive quality you can possess when trying to seduce that most elusive and temperamental life partner – your career.

"If your actions inspire others to dream more, learn more, do more and become more, you are a leader."
— John Quincy Adams

14.2
FINAL WORDS
BY CHRIS CONNELLY, M.B.A.

Cleveland State University, Fall Semester, 2013:

"Remember Andy Kaufman. It's all just performance art," I reminded myself as I walked into MBA 500, Environment of Business, for the first time. I chose a seat on the far periphery of the classroom and reflected on the peculiarly interconnected paths that had led me there. It had been a voyage to rival Ulysses' – fraught with involuntary detours, abrupt dead ends, sinister winds, lurching ghastly creatures, and bold dreams, lured astray by siren songs, only to be dashed like ships upon the rocks. The gods gazed down from the mount, amused.

But it was all finally starting to feel worthwhile. My trials had ultimately infused me with a defiant and somewhat foolhardy self-efficacy. So, I brazenly enrolled in an MBA program as a single father, age 36, with no professional background to speak of. It was a bit of a dare to myself. But it was also a dare to the world at large to let me in.

In my mind I was always an artist first, and every job I ever held was no more than a temporary remedy to ward off complete destitution. I didn't so much date my career. Rather I entered into an endless series of questionable, self-destructive time-for-money relationships out of sheer dependency. When fatherhood in my early 20s brought on heightened responsibilities, I embraced a mindset of "whatever it takes" pragmatism, and worked a series of dirty, dangerous, and sometimes demeaning gigs like so many righteous people do. At the height of the Great Recession, I was laid off from my job as an arborist, the closest I had yet come to a legitimate career. I hastily applied to countless menial positions and quickly discovered that in the current matrix of skills possessed, and job availability, I was essentially unemployable.

Exasperated, and with absolutely nothing to lose, I tried something different. I spent a whirlwind two years reinventing myself, returning to school to complete an undergraduate degree that I had forsaken a decade before. Then, swollen with momentum and newfound confidence, I decided on this next course of action, which probably seemed fairly ludicrous to anyone who had ever known me - an MBA. It was simply the next act of reinvention.

A bit of audacity. Performance art.

Enter Alex.

Despite my cavalier self-assurance, I had my reservations about embarking on this next leg of the expedition. To recap: no business background whatsoever, no professional experience, mid 30s, single father. None of these apprehensions were immediately eased when Alex began to lecture. Honestly, it wasn't a lecture at all. Rather, it was a frank conversation, imbued with a simple, plain-spoken, no-bullshit message:

Suffer no illusions. It's brutal out there. What are you going to do to set yourself apart from the thousands of intelligent, talented, educated young people competing for scarce positions in a down economy?

Alex spoke with the authority of experience. She related to our class many of the same stories and hard-earned lessons found within these pages. She spoke candidly of her personal journey, her experiences in the belly of Corporate America, and her eventual departure from that world to pursue true contentment and autonomy through entrepreneurship, teaching, writing and career coaching.

Let me pause to reemphasize. In my very first class in the MBA program, my professor was telling a room full of would-be executives cautionary tales about the treachery, disloyalty, and instability of Corporate America. She went on to explain how she had been an unfalteringly steadfast servant in that grueling environment for 2 decades, only to lose her job in the market crash of 2008. This shock provided the impetus she needed to make a conscious decision to be her own boss.

This was not at all what I was expecting, but it was a loud wake up call. The thought of facing essentially the same dismal career prospects even after my dramatic reinvention was revolting to me. I immediately resolved to accept Alex's challenge. I would do whatever necessary to set myself apart, and to make it somehow, in my own unique way. Having made this decision, I found the ensuing course to be inordinately enjoyable and provocative.

MBA 500: Business Environment was the obligatory introductory course to the Cleveland State University MBA curriculum. The material covered historically significant cases showcasing the thorny intersections between business, politics, society and media. But far from being a requirement to simply be endured prior to entering the actual program, Alex's class was thought provoking, dynamic, and invaluable to my own understanding of the complex machinations between money and power. The class was fundamentally pro-capitalism, but without any attempt to conceal its darker inclinations. Our discussions that semester were lively and candid explorations of quintessentially American obsessions, the situational elasticity of ethics, and the power of sheer audacity.

We discussed legendary titans of industry whose names stand tall today on America's universities and museums—who also happened to be villainous scoundrels. We learned of billionaire entertainment moguls who drove the pulse of this country's culture, and who had conned and schemed their way into life altering opportunities. We looked unflinchingly at the role of dirty money in the business of politics, Americans' historical love affair with alcohol, tobacco and gambling, and, most notably, the importance of never sparing expenses on one's lawyer or accountant.

Our first assignment in Alex's class was a group presentation on leadership. Paul, myself, and the rest of our team (rather clairvoyantly) decided upon Vladimir Putin as our subject. This was September of 2013. Only three days after our team made this choice, Mr. Putin took out a full-page op-ed in the New York Times criticizing American foreign policy and the idea of American Exceptionalism, and warning against unilateral U.S. military intervention in Syria. Within six months, Putin had staged his own military intervention in Crimea, to administer Russia's annexation of the peninsula by force. As we have all witnessed, these events were mere precursors to Mr. Putin's increasingly bold efforts to restore Russia to global relevance and influence by undermining Western authority and institutions at every turn, including a ridiculously brazen (and by all appearances successful) effort to influence the outcome of the most fundamental element of American democracy – a presidential election.

Alex absolutely loved our team's choice of subject. She wasn't condoning Machiavellian political strategy (or his KGB grooming) per say. She knew our team had understood that the assignment was about leadership, not some vague criteria for sainthood. We had recognized in Putin the invaluable worth of audacity and calculated risk as traits of those who wish to change the world, even if at the time there was no real way of knowing the extent to which he would soon impose his will upon the shaping of our current global affairs.

With all of the transformative changes that have since materialized, both in the world, and in my own life, it is difficult to fathom that only three years have passed. As I read Date Your Career, it was like being transported back into Alex's classroom as a contemplative, first semester MBA student and hearing all of her accumulated wisdom again for the first time. The no-nonsense, straightforward advice, delivered in her singular voice throughout the pages of this book echoed much of what I was quietly soaking up like a sponge on the far right side of her classroom in that fall of 2013.

As I was recently paging through my notes from MBA 500, this jumped out at me: "You need laser focus to get there and succeed. Be aggressive. Act like you belong. But watch your back." Yes, that was actually in quotes. That was Alex talking to our class, seemingly channeling my firebrand high school basketball coach, and a wise guy Scorsese character simultaneously.

Incidentally, I have also been fortunate enough to be able to enlist Alex's services as a career coach. I can attest that the principles in this book pertaining to the job search, resumes, and interviewing are directly mirrored in the approach that Alex takes in her personal consulting, and that in my experience they are very effective. I should mention that in addition to being an MBA student with a focus on Finance, I was concurrently a bartender and a college radio DJ at Cleveland State. I may not be the first person to simultaneously perform these three roles, but I imagine it is a fairly elite club. Within several months of receiving Alex's coaching, I was hired, straight out of graduate school to my first professional position. Alex helped me to tell my unique story, and to stitch together the disparate experiences that had brought me to her class, and to illustrate my strengths in a way that hiring managers could understand and appreciate.

Now, for the first time having finally arrived the point of career stability, I feel genuinely liberated to dedicate more time to my creative pursuits, including writing. In this capacity as well, no one has encouraged me as much as Alex. She recently reminded me that we are overdue for a cultural renaissance and a new Age of Reason. It was implicit that I need to be a participant. Perhaps someday soon I will feel confident enough to throw myself headlong into working for myself full time. I'm not quite there yet. I'm a late-bloomer after all. Baby steps. However, I know very well that I need to "Be the captain, or someone else will."

I consider myself very fortunate to have been placed in that particular MBA 500 class. I learned that rather than a life sentence in obedient servitude chasing a prestigious job title, an MBA education can be a limitless career toolkit to cultivate inventiveness, freedom, and yes, audacity. The rogue in me really likes that. Equally important, I learned that business and art were never mutually exclusive. In fact, they have always been perfect partners.

I was a non-traditional MBA student and Alex was a non-traditional MBA instructor. It was a providential encounter. One of the sort that can dramatically alter the trajectory of a career and a life. I will always be thankful that I accepted my own dare. Not coincidentally, so did the world at large.

Talent works together.
Ego just shouts.
- #CreativeCadence

#DateYourCareer

SECTION 3 – MEET THE WRITERS

"Even though no one admits it, writers are leaders in their communities."
– Pramoedya Ananta Toer

ABOUT THE AUTHOR

Alexsandra (Alex) Sukhoy, M.B.A. is Founder and Career Coach of her content and consulting company Creative Cadence LLC. Alex is also Mom to David, her high-energy toddler and the miracle of her life. He is her toughest CEO.

She holds a B.A. in Communication with a minor in Art from DePaul University and an M.B.A. in Marketing and in Competitive Strategy from the Simon Business School. Over the course of two decades she climbed the Corporate America Ladder, earning numerous leadership roles at global organizations, including American Greetings, Rand McNally and VTech, launching thousands of profitable products and managing cross-functional teams, all the while presenting to key senior executives.

Alex loves integrating her business savvy and her creativity to help people and companies achieve their professional goals. She has been profiled in *Bloomberg Businessweek* and featured in numerous publications, including *International Business Times*, *Newsweek Japan* and *U.S. News and World Report*, as well as invited by various universities and community organizations to guest lecture on steering one's career.

She holds an Adjunct Faculty position at Cleveland State University's Monte Ahuja College of Business, growing her 1000+ undergrad and graduate students' understanding of marketing and the business environment. For over five years Alex wrote the Career ToolBox column for award-winning CoolCleveland. She also taught at the Journalism and Media Arts departments at the Cuyahoga Community College and for two years she actively contributed movie industry insight, producer interviews and film critiques to *Film Slate Magazine*. In 2015 she was a TCM Top 10 Film Noir Twitter Script Submission Finalist, as then reviewed by Ed Burns.

Alex's books, all anchored in the struggle and hope of the human condition, including *Diary of the Dumped: 30 Days From Break Up to Breakthrough*, have sold all over the globe. *The '90s: Diary of a Mess*, reached #14 on the Amazon Kindle Poetry Anthologies Best Seller List. Her two earlier novellas, *Chatroom to Bedroom: Chicago*, and its follow up, *Chatroom to Bedroom: Rochester, NY*, continue to sell on Amazon.

Date Your Career: The Longest Relationship of Your Life is her first business book. A couple of the essays in this book were picked up by the *HuffPost*.

Alex thrives on travel, befriending people of all backgrounds and cultures, creating an extended family that spans the globe. In 2014 she partook in a five-month travel adventure that included living and writing in Dublin, Ireland, where she got to meet the now late John Hurt. At heart, she's a storyteller.

FOREWORD

THOMAS MULREADY

As creator of Cool Networks LLC, Mulready leads a multimedia network utilizing blogs, podcasts, videos, e-blasts and mobile apps to promote economic development, arts, culture and technology in Northeast Ohio under the flagship CoolCleveland.

After creating the Performance Art Festival+Archives, he co-founded the Ingenuity Festival of Art and Technology, and has served as Senior Vice President of National City Bank and worked at Management Recruiters International, Richardson-Vicks, and Campbell Soup.

He's played drums with Cats On Holiday and Vanity Crash, presented his performance art in New York and Paris, and served as a Senior Research Consultant in the United Kingdom. His multimedia presentations on David Bowie, Glam and The Beatles have been presented at universities, jazz clubs and aquariums.

CONTRIBUTORS

BRYAN CEJA, M.B.A.

California native born at the head of the Gen X wave. Deeply influenced by the varied music of the 1970's and 80's.

Lived the classic dual-culture life of most Mexican-Americans; one foot in each culture with the adaptive personality necessary to thrive in both.

On my own since I was 18 and became a retail rat working two to three jobs in Los Angeles and San Francisco, including a famous video store in West Hollywood due to my love of movies with a big celebrity clientele.

Found a home at Rand McNally due to my love of maps. I dated that career in marketing and the technological revolution dumped us both. Found a second home at Telemundo marketing and working with the Latino community, my second passion, and the big recession scaled that back.

I am back in the retail world; a classic Gen X rebounder story.

Looking for my next chapter. I have a BS in multi-cultural marketing from DePaul University, including studying in Buenos Aires and Santiago.

I have an MBA from Grand Canyon University.

CHRISTOPHER CONNELLY, M.B.A.

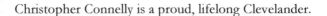

Christopher Connelly is a proud, lifelong Clevelander.

Five years ago, he was making minimum wage working at the pizza shop at the end of his street after being laid off from his job as an arborist. Despite several shambolic attempts at college, he had never advanced beyond his high school education.

Now, having earned an undergraduate degree in Political Science/International Relations and an M.B.A., he resides in Dayton where he works in procurement of goods and services for the U.S. Air Force. He still drives up to Cleveland every weekend to be at home with his loved ones.

A confirmed rock and roll apostle, Christopher is also the former host of The Fallout Shelter, a weekly college radio show that aired every Tuesday while he was a graduate student at Cleveland State University. The show explored the fringes of the new American and Global underground; introducing listeners to a highly-curated selection of newly released sonic mayhem.

Acting on the advice prescribed by Alex in Part 1 of her chapter on entrepreneurship, Mr. Connelly is preparing to register his first domain name, to use as a launch pad for his innumerable future contributions to the New Cultural Renaissance.

ERIC DUNN, M.B.A., OSM

Eric Dunn is an analyst with a background in information systems, risk analysis, and process improvement. He holds an MBA with a specialization in Operations and Supply Chain Management from the Monte Ahuja College of Business at Cleveland State University. In 2009, Eric graduated Cum Laude with a Bachelor of Arts in Psychology from Cleveland State University. In 2006, he earned an associate of arts in English from Cuyahoga Community College, also Cum Laude.

In 2007, Eric earned a lifetime membership into the Golden Key International Honor society. In the spring of 2009, he was inducted into Psi Chi, the international honor society in Psychology. In 2015, Eric received membership into Beta Gamma Sigma, the international honor society in Business.

Ever the entrepreneur, in 1997, at the age of 14, Eric started the "Attitude Era" newsletter which would later be acquired by WrestlingGames.com. The successful videogame website would go on to be a leader in providing wrestling game information and content on the web, attracting millions of views on a monthly basis. Currently Eric is working to launch two new business ventures, Evans & Dunn LLC, which is focused on providing business solution delivery; and Peake Fitness, which is dedicated to helping those struggling with weight management accomplish their goals.

Eric currently resides in Cleveland, Ohio where he was born and raised. He is an avid sneaker head with a collection that has rapidly over taken his living space. In his free time, he enjoys working out, traveling, and spending time (or what's left of it) with family and friends.

Eric also provides mentorship to young professionals looking to navigate the complexities of the work, life, and school balance.

PAUL IBRAHIM, M.B.A.

Born and raised in Cleveland, OH, Paul Ibrahim is married to the love of his life, Mallorie.

Together they have two dogs, two cats, and are expecting their first child. The dogs are brother and sister rescues, as are the cats.

Paul obtained his Bachelor's in Engineering and MBA from Cleveland State University. During his MBA studies, he met this book's author, Alexsandra Sukhoy.

Paul has worked at Parker Hannifin, Philips Healthcare, and Ford Motor Company in his career.

He is equally at home hunting in the wilderness of Montana, hiking the Cleveland Metroparks with his Akita, Zeus, or attending a Tchaikovsky piece put on by the world-leading Cleveland Symphony Orchestra.

Paul is outspoken and animated, and has a deep passion for history, his family, and pushing his physical limits daily.

DEENA NYER MENDLOWITZ

Deena has a Bachelor's Degree in Communications from Bradley University and a Masters in severe depression.

She is a freelance writer, has done a shit ton of stuff in the non-profit world, and has also worked as an on-staff humor writer for American Greetings.

Deena is an improviser who trained at The Second City Cleveland and at both The Second City and Annoyance Theater in Chicago. Deena has performed with a number of comedy groups on stage and also for corporate brainstorms, non-profit events, and festivals (in other words, she's for hire.)

Deena is the creator of This Improvised Life, a part improvised, part written story-telling hour. She is also the co-creator of a kind, funny, awesome, nine year old boy who has a huge Star Wars collection, over 33 hats, and constantly crushes her in foosball. He would also like you to know they have named all the foosball players.

This is Deena's second written contribution to one of Alex's books, the first reflecting about her memories and experiences in Chicago in *The 90s: Diary of a Mess.*

Check out Deena's website: funnelcakesnotincluded.com

RACHEL PANKIW, M.B.A.

Rachel Pankiw earned a BS in Advertising with a minor in Public Relations from Kent State University. As a former journalism major turned marketing professional, she has developed unique skillsets in content marketing, media relations, and marketing communications strategy.

She recently graduated from Cleveland State with an MBA in Marketing and a Graduate Certificate in Marketing Analytics, while working as a marketing specialist and business advisor for The Small Business Development Center.

She currently works as a Marketing Communications Manager for Speedeon Data, a marketing analytics/market research firm in Cleveland.

KATIE KARSTEN

Katie Karsten is the Managing Director at K2 Communications Group, located in Chicago.

A Communications graduate of North Park University, Katie is an award-winning and high-energy Communicator and Storyteller with agency and production expertise. She's held multiple media roles with industry-leading organizations, including Blue Chip Marketing Worldwide, Curro, Rankin & Williams, Dolores Kohl Education Foundation, WTTW/Chicago PBS and J. Walter Thompson.

You can learn more about Katie and connect with her at linkedin.com/in/katiekarsten/

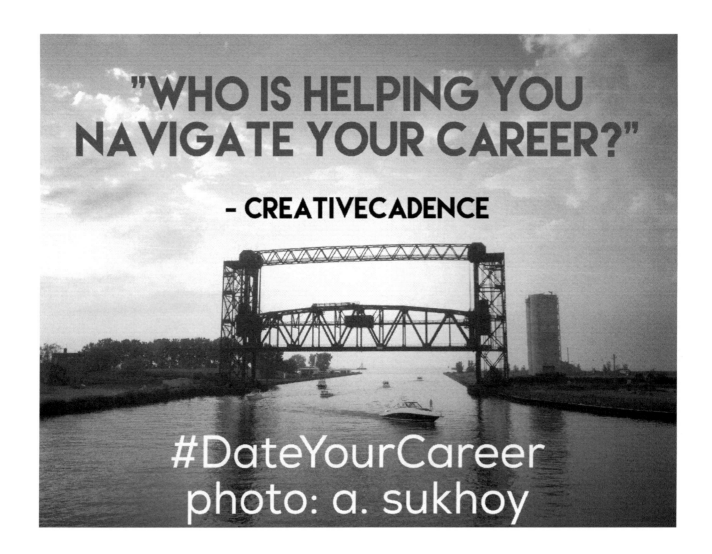

"WHO IS HELPING YOU NAVIGATE YOUR CAREER?"

- CREATIVECADENCE

#DateYourCareer
photo: a. sukhoy

Made in the USA
San Bernardino, CA
15 June 2017